The New Americans
Recent Immigration and American Society

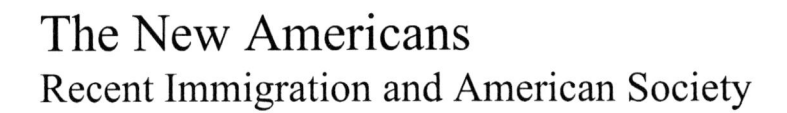

Edited by
Carola Suárez-Orozco and Marcelo Suárez-Orozco

A Series from LFB Scholarly

Changing Gender Roles
Brazilian Immigrant Families in the U.S.

Sylvia Duarte Dantas DeBiaggi

LFB Scholarly Publishing LLC
New York 2002

Copyright © 2002 by LFB Scholarly Publishing LLC

All rights reserved.

Library of Congress Cataloging-in-Publication Data

DeBiaggi, Sylvia Duarte Dantas.
 Changing gender roles : recent immigration and American society / DeBiaggi, Sylvia Duarte Dantas ; edited by Carola Suarez-Orozco and Marcelo Suarez-Orozco.
    p. cm. -- (The new Americans)
 Includes bibliographical references and index.
   ISBN 1-931202-19-2 (acid-free paper)
 1. Brazilian Americans--Social conditions. 2. Brazilian Americans--Ethnic identity. 3. Immigrants--United States--Social conditions. 4. Husbands--United States--Social conditions. 5. Wives--United States--Social conditions. 6. Family--United States. 7. Sex role--United States. 8. Man-woman relationships--United States. I. Title. II. New Americans (LFB Scholarly Publishing LLC)
  E184.B68 D43 2001
  305.86'98073--dc21

2001005074

ISBN 1-931202-19-2

Printed on acid-free 250-year-life paper.

Manufactured in the United States of America.

Table of Contents

Introduction	1
Chapter 1: Brazilian Emigration	7
Characteristics of Brazilian Immigrants	10
Studies about Brazilians in the U.S	13
Reasons for Immigrating	18
Chapter 2: Acculturation	23
Chapter 3: Gender Roles	39
Gender Roles: A Historical Review	41
Gender Roles: Division of Labor	43
Gender Roles: Attitudes	44
Gender Roles and Marital Satisfaction	48
Gender Roles in Brazilian Society	50
Gender Roles: Division of Labor and Attitudes in Brazil	51
Role Conflict: Gender Role in Immigration	56
Chapter 4: Method	61
Participants	61
Study Design and Procedures	64
Measures	65
Chapter 5: Results	73

Chapter 6: Discussion	99
Appendix A: Consent Form	113
Appendix B: Questionnaire	117
References	141
Index	161

List of Figures

Figure 1: Cluster Analysis Grouping of Couples Based
on Acculturation Factors   89

List of Tables

Table 1: Range, Mean, Standard Deviations, and Median of Husbands and Wives' Score ... 74

Table 2: Summary of First Regression Analysis of Variables Predicting Wives' Marital Satisfaction ... 82

Table 3: Summary of Regression Analysis of Gender Role Attitude of More Acculturated Husbands Predicting Wives Marital satisfaction ... 83

Table 4: Summary of Regression Analysis of Gender Role Attitude of Less Acculturated Husbands Predicting Wives Marital Satisfaction ... 84

Table 5: Summary of Second Regression Analysis of Variables Predicting Husbands Marital Satisfaction ... 85

Table 6: Summary of Third Regression Analysis of Variables Predicting Wives Marital Satisfaction ... 86

Table 7: Four cluster Groups and Means of Acculturation Factors ... 90

Table 8: Mean of Cluster groups of Couples on Their Marital satisfaction, Household, Childcare, Feminine Tasks and Masculine Tasks ... 93

Acknowledgements

I am very grateful for the financial support that came from two awards I was given during my graduate years. First from the Brazilian government's Coordenação de Aperfeiçoamento de Pessoal de Nível Superior (CAPES) which supported me for four years and then from the Clara Mayo Award at Boston University's Psychology Department for my research project which supported me for a year making my data collection and analysis possible.

There are many people I would like to thank for their help with the present research. Professor Leslie Brody whose guidance, encouragement and instruction kept me going and focused. Professor Amy Sales for guidance and precious feedback. Professor Deborah Belle and Professor Marcelo Suarez-Orozco who provided me with important bibliographical references. Professors Anne Copeland and Kathleen Malley-Morrison for revisions and comments.

For their statistical expertise I thank professor Gabriella Stagnhause, Patricia Hilst and Carter Yeager.

Within the Brazilian community of Boston I would like to thank the active leaders: Heloisa Souza from the Brazilian Women's Group, Graciane, Luciane and Regina from MAPS who assisted me with questionnaire matters and recruitment of interviewees. In that same line, I would like to thank Father Roque, Minister Samuel and my friend Silvia Villace. Further, friends supported me and had me at their houses when I no longer lived in Boston: Sharon Bernanke and Paul Bricky, Wellington Cardoso, Cecilia Shutz and Eliane Rubinstein. Also, Wilson Flanders for information about the community, and in Brazil, Professors Geraldo Paiva and Eva Alterman Blay for support, Cristina Martes and Elisa Sassaki for bibliographical references and Maria Helena Saleme for special support.

Further I am deeply grateful to all the families I interviewed and who shared with me intimate aspects of their immigrant family life. I wish all the best for each and one of them. I consider them heroes. They left everything they had behind and came to an unknown place many times not knowing the language, bringing their children to fight for a better family life. As one of the wives said and asked me to mention her statement in my dissertation, "If we could have a good life condition in Brazil we would not be here". She was sad but at the same time proud of her achievements in the new land. Many expressed the same thought. Immigration is a complex matter. I hope this study can contribute to immigrant's family life by showing that gender role changes instead of a threat can enhance family quality in the new country.

I want to thank my parents Caio and Bene, for their constant involvement, concern and real support, my brother Luis, for his interest on the theme and exchange of ideas, my sister Monica, for support, my parents in-law, Enaura and Emer, for support and encouragement and my sister in-law Enali (Leca) for important geographical data on Brazil.

Finally, I would like to dedicate this book to my husband, Emerson, and to my daughter, Gabriella (Biba) with lots of love.

Introduction

The current study explores the relation of acculturation to gender role attitudes and behavior among Brazilian immigrant families in the United States. Further, these processes (acculturation, gender role attitudes and behavior) are investigated in relation to marital adjustment. Brazilians are a fairly recent and little studied immigrant population to the United States (Assis, 1995; Bicalho, 1989; DeBiaggi, 1992, 1996; Goza, 1994; Margolis,1989, 1994; Martes, 2000, 2001; Ribeiro, 1999; Sales, 1992, 1999). Estimates show 800,000 Brazilians in the United States (Salgado & Carelli, 2001). Moreover, emigration is a recent phenomenon in Brazil, a country that previously had a reputation for receiving immigrants from other parts of the world. Brazilians in the U.S. add to the Latino population. However, although Brazil is a Latin American nation, there are differences and particularities that set Brazilian culture apart from other Latin cultures. One major difference, for instance, is language: Brazilians, unlike most South and Central Americans, speak Portuguese and not Spanish. Also, Latinos are a very diverse group and the Hispanic categorization is usually misleading, since it considers different populations as if they were a monolithic block. As Suarez-Orozco and Suarez-Orozco (1995) explain "Although they share some characteristics, Latinos are a diverse demographic and sociocultural population" (p.4). It is like considering Americans from the U.S. the same as Canadians because they both represent the Anglo-American culture of the Americas. Thus, when looking at Brazilians we are necessarily speaking of "a new ingredient in the melting pot" as Margolis (1994) states. In that sense, the present study's findings present similarities and differences from studies of other Latin populations.

Immigration is a complex matter fraught with psychological implications. It does not involve simply dislocation from one place to another. It can also involve the loss of all that the country of origin represents: native language, common cultural habits, rules and norms, social support of extended or near family, friends, acquaintances, well-known environment, and so on. Studies have shown that immigration entails a process of cultural transformation or acculturation. Thus, immigration is an uprooting experience accompanied by an acculturation process that involves changes in one's value system, attitudes, behavior, way of life, and relationship patterns. It is important to note that the term acculturation here, as it will be explained later, does not mean assimilation as in more traditional perspectives of cross-cultural studies. It is conceptualized as a multidimensional process in which both the individual's culture of origin and the host culture play a significant role in the adjustment process.

An earlier qualitative study of Brazilian immigrant families in Boston revealed that changing gender roles within the family structure constitute a major theme of immigrant adjustment (DeBiaggi, 1992). The disruption of a previous gender role pattern constitutes one of the great

Introduction 3

challenges Brazilian families face in their move to the North American sociocultural environment. Gender role attitudes and behaviors are some of the important factors involved in immigrants' adjustment to the new society. The family system faces changes and challenges in its previously established gender role behaviors and attitudes. It loses the predictability of its past roles, which helped to stabilize family interactions (Cornille & Brotherton, 1993). Such changes are a factor in immigrant marital dissolution.

However, most studies on immigration and acculturation have looked at the immigrants' experience on an individual basis (Ghaffarian, 1987; Hanassab, 1991; Torres-Matrullo, 1976, 1980). These studies have indicated a change in the relationship between acculturation and changes in gender role attitudes towards a more liberal view of women's roles. Fewer studies have focused on the family as a unit of analysis (Kirkland, 1984; Rueschenberg & Buriel, 1989; Woon, 1986). Further, many studies that address the family or aim to explain family changes in gender role patterns rarely include couples that are married or live together or consider only women's views about the couple (Guendelman, 1987; Hartman & Hartman, 1986; Landale, 1993; Melville, 1978; Meredith & Rowe, 1986; Pessar, 1984). Therefore, the present research aims at studying the immigrant family unit by gathering data from married couples. The researcher interviewed fifty Brazilians immigrant families in the greater Boston area. Most of the interviews were in the respondents' homes, where the family shares their daily immigrant life. Couples had at least one child, had lived an average of twelve years together, and had lived an average of seven years in the U.S.. In most couples both husbands and wives were employed. Most of the wives worked as domestic house cleaners for American families, as did some of their husbands. The American household became a comparative scenario through which wives and husbands apprehended a way of organizing life that is different from their own.

By looking at how Brazilians' acculturation relates to their gender roles in the U.S., this research also contributes to the study of gender issues among Brazilians and non-middle class white American women, around whom most previous studies have been centered. Further, studies on women's issues in Brazil started to receive scholarly attention only during the mid to late seventies, later than in the U.S. and Western Europe (Costa, Barroso and Sarti, 1985; Hahner, 1984). Gender role issues among Brazilians need to be more widely addressed and understood.

This study examines how the interaction of cultural changes and changes in gender roles influence immigrant couples' relationships. The present work contributes to the understanding of the acculturation process of immigrants by looking at previously understudied family processes, by using multivariate models of both gender roles and acculturation and also by studying their effect on the marital relationship.

The book begins with a description of Brazilians in the new country, particularly in the greater Boston area, and reasons for their move to the U.S.. Then, the concept of acculturation and the factors involved in that process are addressed in the second chapter. In the third chapter, a description of the concept of gender roles and its relation to marital satisfaction in North American culture, and a summary of gender roles in Brazilian society is presented. Further, findings of studies that relate changing gender roles to immigration are described. Next, the methodology of the present study is described in chapter four, and the

Introduction 5

results obtained are addressed in chapter five. A discussion of the study is then presented in the final chapter.

In summary, this book explores the lives of Brazilian immigrants, including the relationships among acculturation, gender roles and marital satisfaction. The main questions are: 1) How does acculturation relate to gender roles? and 2) How do acculturation and gender roles relate to marital satisfaction?

CHAPTER 1
Brazilian Emigration

Emigration is a fairly recent phenomenon in Brazil, a country that previously had a reputation for receiving immigrants from other parts of the world. As Bassanezi (1995) says, Brazil's immigration history actually begins with the Portuguese, who in 1500 colonized the land by military and economic appropriation. As one Brazilian song says "The Indians were already here".

Further, the Portuguese introduced forced labor on the plantations to develop crops for export. During the three centuries ending in 1850 about four million Africans entered Brazil as slaves. Portuguese government policies attracted other foreigners, including Germans and Italians. However, the great surge of international immigration to Brazil occurred after the end of slavery. During the 19th and 20th centuries Portuguese, Italians, Spaniards, Germans, Japanese and people from other nations immigrated to Brazil attracted by the labor opportunities the country offered. Statistical data show that from 1872 to 1972, 5.350.889 immigrants entered the country, mostly from Portugal and Italy but also from Spain, Germany, Japan, and other countries (Bassanezi, 1995). Indeed, although only 248.007 Japanese immigrated to Brazil, today Brazil hosts the largest community of Japanese and their descendents outside Japan. More recently, immigration from Korea, China and Bolivia is significant, adding to the current estimate of 1 million foreigners living in Brazil ("Brasil continua", 06/18/00).

However, at the end of the 20th century the reverse process began: Brazilians left their country in search of a better life in other lands. Brazil, according to the last census done in the year two thousand (IBGE 2000), has a population of 171,684,668 and is South America's most populous nation. Demographers showed that during the 1980s there was an exodus for the first time in Brazilian history. Until then, emigration was insignificant and therefore never considered when counting the country's population. At present, about 1% of Brazilians has left the country. Estimates from the Itamaraty, the Brazilian Ministry of Foreign Affairs, indicate that 1.900.000 Brazilians live abroad (Salgado & Carelli, 2001) The number of Brazilians living in other countries increased approximately 20% each year (Sales, 1991). The United States, Paraguay, Japan and Europe constitute the main hosts of this recent emigrant population.

The majority of these Brazilians are in the United States, primarily in New York, Boston, and Miami. There are no official data on how many Brazilians live in the United States, since the official immigration data does not account for undocumented aliens. Estimates from the Itamaraty, the Brazilian Ministry of Foreign Affairs, show in 1996, 610,130 Brazilians in the United States with 230,000 in New York, 150,000 in Boston, 130,000 in Miami and others in Washington, Houston, San Francisco, Los Angeles, Chicago and San Juan (Klintowitz, 4/3/96).

Brazilian Emigration 9

In 1990, the U.S. Immigration and Naturalization Service admitted 377.284 non-immigrants from Brazil, the majority of them tourists (286.450). In the same year, 2.541 Brazilians attained permanent resident status. The majority of them had entered as tourists and some, even, illegally. In that same year in May, 7,759 Brazilian applied for American citizenship. The majority applied under the Seasonal Agricultural Workers (SAW) program, part of the "amnesty" provided by the Immigration Reform and Control Act of 1986. In Massachusetts, in 1990, approximately 1.200 applied for legalization under the SAW program (DeBiaggi, 1992).

In 1998, the U.S. Immigration and Naturalization Service admitted 934,679 non-immigrants from Brazil, mostly tourists (779,000). Most entered Florida (402,330) and New York (201,158). In the same year, 4,401 Brazilian immigrants were admitted and 1,927 Brazilians naturalized as Americans. At the beginning of the 1990s the number naturalized every year was only in the hundreds, but by the middle of the decade it was in the thousands with a peak of 2,685 in 1996. Moreover, 86 Brazilian orphans were adopted in 1998, of which 24 were between 5 to 9 years old and 26 were over 9 years of age. Curiously, the case of a Brazilian boy living in the U.S. since the age of 8 and adopted by an American couple, was focus of attention of the Brazilian media. The "boy", now 22 years old, was deported to Brazil, although he no longer spoke Portuguese or had any relatives or friends to help him. In the U.S., he had been caught selling marijuana to a police informant. His naturalization had not been concluded when he was arrested in 1997 ("Jovem deportado", 2000). In the American legal system, adoption does not involve automatic naturalization, only after five years of residence may the parents file for naturalization of their adopted offspring (Calligaris, 1999).

In 1989, social service workers estimated that Boston sheltered about 25.000 undocumented Brazilians (Blake, 11/6/89). However, a 1992 estimate by the Archdiocese of Boston (Franklin, 2/3/92), data still considered valid by Itamaraty and most demographers, calculated 150,000 Brazilians in the five counties of the archdiocese, six times the statewide estimates done the previous year.

These vast numbers of Brazilians abroad forced the government's Ministry of Foreign Affairs to change its priority from external commerce to that of supporting Brazilian citizens in other countries through the "Programa de apoio aos brasileiros no exterior" (Support Program to Brazilians Abroad; "Emigrante" 2000; Ribeiro, 1999). The government also began to encourage the creation of citizen councils around the world to function as a link between communities and the consulates ("Emigrante" 2000). In 1995-97 forty citizen councils were created, in Boston, New York, Miami, Los Angeles, San Francisco, Washington, Chicago, Houston, and other cities (Martes, 2001). To provide further support to Brazilian immigrants and to help them maintain cultural ties to Brazil the government is providing libraries with books by Brazilian authors, validating diplomas and offering resources for schooling in the Brazilian educational system abroad ("Emigrante" 2000).

Characteristics of Brazilian Immigrants

At the beginning of this exodus the emigrating population was predominantly composed of males, at a ratio of three or four men to each woman, but at the end of the 1980s and beginning of the 1990s more women and families began to emigrate (Franklin, 2/3/92).

The Connection Governador Valadares-Boston:
The majority of the Brazilian migrants to Boston came from the state of Minas Gerais in south central Brazil. The typical Brazilian immigrant in Boston is from one town in Minas Gerais, Governador Valadares, and its surroundings. Governador Valdares is a city of 246,944 people (IBGE, 2000) located 303 kilometers from Belo Horizonte, the capital of the state of Minas Gerais. The city is a regional economic center for the east and northeast part of the state as well as for the neighboring state of Espírito Santo (Assis, 1995). Historically, the American connection with Governador Valdares dates from World War II when American airplanes took off regularly from Governador Valadares carrying mica, then an essential material for making radios. The connection was maintained even after the war, since the city became a semiprecious stone trading center for many American businessmen (Brooke, 11/30/90). During the 1960s, unemployment increased after loggers cut down the tropical forest around the region. Then, young men started making the ten hour bus trip to Rio de Janeiro which was later be replaced by the journey to the U.S. (Brooke, 11/30/90). The first emigrants during the 1960s wanted to stay temporarily in the U.S., to save enough money to return and then open their own business. Or, they were eager for a new adventure. Others worked under seasonal programs offered by the American government and today, these pioneers in immigration own gas stations, buildings and land in Governador Valadares (Assis, 1995). But their number during the 60s was not demographically significant.

Social scientists address the connection between the two cities as having created a "culture of out-migration" in Valadares, a term applied to communities that have an established pattern of international migration (Margolis, 1994). In Valadares the prospect of going to the United States or knowing someone who has gone there is part of daily life. Many residents receive remittances from relatives in the States or administer immigrants' local real estate investments and other enterprises with dollars sent from abroad. Further, other aspects make the connection to the U.S. evident even to a passerby: tourist agencies focusing on travel to the U.S., currency exchanges and local newspapers with columns on issues pertaining to immigration (Assis, 1995; Margolis, 1994). *States News* is a newspaper written for and by immigrants to the U.S. but published in Governador Valdares. More than 40,000 copies of *States News* are distributed every week around eastern Minas with advertisements of homes and mall space in Brazil as well as Brazilian services in the United States. As Millman (1997) notes, the newspaper is "a printed form of the traditional immigrant grapevine, a sophisticated effort to exploit the millions of 'Vala-dolares' entering Minas every month" (p.213).

Further, not only are the townspeople exposed to a diversity of information about emigration, but also the remittances provided by relatives and friends enable the move. As Margolis argues, "a culture of out-migration provides both the ideology and the material basis – in the form of remittances from relatives abroad – that enhance the possibility of emigration for people from a wide range of backgrounds" (p.96). According to a study conducted by Soares (1999), from 1984 to 1993 emigrants were responsible for more then a third of the town's real state investments, equivalent to $153,727,000. Currently, most of the townspeople have a relative in the United States, mainly in Boston (Sales, 1992). Roughly half of the immigrant Brazilian population in Boston is from Valadares (Franklin, 2/3/92; Martes, 1999).

Studies about Brazilians in the U.S.

Scholars in sociology, anthropology, and psychology at American and Brazilian universities have written on Brazilians in the United States. In the U.S., Goza (1994) presented a sociological case study of recent immigration and adjustment by Brazilians to Canada and the U.S. He found several contrasts between the two countries. In the first phase of his study in 1989, 450 household interviews were conducted in a municipality of the state of Minas Gerais. Over 71% of these households had friends or relatives residing abroad. The immigrants themselves were then located and interviewed in two cities in both Canada and the U.S. Each sample consisted of 195 Brazilian-born residents. In addition to socio-demographic variables, employment status, educational activities prior to departure, social-economic status (SES) of the migrant's family, employment history in the U.S., migration network, remittances, and plans for the future were addressed. Over 20% of both samples were from Governador Valadares and surrounding cities. Their educational level of over ten years of formal education was high compared to the general Brazilian population. Results showed that most Brazilians immigrate as family units. Despite similar SES of Canadian and U.S. immigrants, their present and future plans were different. In the U.S. most Brazilians seemed to be target earners: even if it took them fifteen years to reach their savings goals they planned to return to Brazil. In Canada, on the other hand, significantly more immigrants wanted to stay permanently. Goza related the wish to stay in the country to Brazilians being more involved in improving their English and professional skills in Canada, but admits that the phenomenon may be limited to the sample population and city chosen for the study.

An ethnography of Brazilians in New York by Margolis (1994), thoroughly depicts that immigrant population of the city. The two-phased study, began in 1988 and 89, when she conducted fifty-three informal, open-ended interviews with Brazilian immigrants, including Brazilian consular officers and store owners. Then in 1990, 100 Brazilian immigrants were interviewed and responded to a questionnaire covering most aspects of their immigrant life such as how the decision to immigrate was made, how they came to the U.S., their first days in New York, the types of jobs they had and prior work histories. Based on property ownership, occupational and educational data of the informants and their parents, Margolis found that 11% were from the upper middle-class, 30% were middle-class, 50% lower middle-class, and only 9% lower class. In Brazil 60% of the population is concentrated in the two lowest classes, but in this immigrant sample in New York only about 10% belongs to these categories. Unlike those headed to Boston, the majority, 46%, in New York had attended a university and of those 31% had graduated. In 1990 in Brazil, 28% of the Brazilian population complete secondary school and only 12% went on to higher education, in sharp contrast to Margoli's sample. Brazilian males monopolize the shoe shining business in New York and occupy other service sector jobs such as bus boy and dishwasher in restaurants of the city. The women, on the other hand, work as baby-sitters, live-in or live-out maids and go-go dancers.

Heisler (1995), in a study about the demographic characteristics of the Brazilian community in East Boston and their perceived health needs and utilization of health services, interviewed 100 Brazilians. The majority of the sample was from Minas Gerais and about half had completed high school. The study concludes that a culturally sensitive and Portuguese-speaking staff is important for Brazilians' health care.

Moretto (1991) conducted a study with the aim of identifying the pre- and post-immigration stresses and needs of Brazilians in the greater Boston area. Most of the one hundred subjects were originally from Governador Valadares. For them separation from family and friends in Brazil was a potential source of stress. Moreover, the subjects indicated great dissatisfaction with the quality of support received from their fellow countrymen. Instead of finding support they reported being exploited or taken advantage of by other Brazilians.

In a previous qualitative study (DeBiaggi, 1992), I extensively interviewed five Brazilian immigrant families in the Greater Boston area. The interviews were based on a questionnaire addressing immigrant family life, community involvement, household activities, and child rearing. Of the common themes, gender role conflicts was the most salient. Other themes were the stress of separation from the extended family, disappointment in not meeting their financial goals, and lack of social support among Brazilian immigrants. In dealing with female and male role, disparities patterns of relationship emerge among the immigrant couples (DeBiaggi, 1996).

Further, Millman (1997), an international journalist, in *The Other Americans* writes about the new business strategies and business synergies brought by immigrants and how they merge into American culture. Millman devotes one chapter to Brazilians in Framingham, Massachusetts. He describes the sending and receiving towns of Governador Valadares and Framingham in Massachusetts and discusses how migration changes both places. He argues that the influx of Brazilians in Framingham has added economically and culturally to the town.

The first Brazilian book on immigration to the U.S. is by Bicalho (1989). His work is a mixture of fiction and fact based on the stories of immigrants he met during his stay in the United States in 1989. He interviewed 81 Brazilian immigrants living in Framingham and presents demographic data and facts about their immigration. The majority lived in Minas Gerais before heading to the United States; 74% of them were from the city of Governador Valadares and surrounding towns, and 53% of the sample had graduated from **high** school.

Sales (1992) analyses the Brazilian exodus and in another sociological study focuses in the Brazilian population in the town of Framingham (Sales, 1999). There are an estimated 6,000 Brazilians in the town, but the author estimates 2,400 Brazilians there, based on a reading of the telephone book. The study is based on informal qualitative interviews and focus groups with Brazilians of the local Catholic and Protestant churches. Also included are seven narratives of Brazilian immigrant women. Sales (1999), indicates how Brazilians, after overstaying the time of their original plans to reside in the U.S., start to constitute an ethnic enclave with their own organizations, religious gatherings and ethnic stores. Further, the author concludes that Brazilians begin to build their ethnic identity based on their own self-concept and also on how they are described as hard-workers and entrepreneurs by the local American press.

Assis (1995) conducted a qualitative study based on letters sent to Governador Valadares by Brazilians in the U.S., and 33 semi-structured interviews, of which 15 were with Brazilian immigrants in the U.S., while the others were with relatives or return migrants in Governador Valadares. The study indicates how a migration culture was constructed in the city forming the connection between Governador Valadares and the U.S.

In an anthropological study of Brazilians in San Francisco, Ribeiro (1999) analyses the festivals in the town that affirm Brazilian identity, such as Brazilian ethnic restaurants, night clubs, bars, music, and religious ceremonies. Unlike on the East Coast, in San Francisco the majority of Brazilians, according to consulate data, come from the state of Goiás in mid-western Brazil. The author indicates that in spite of their regional background, Brazilian's cultural manifestations in San Francisco express well-known national symbols.

In a sociological study of Brazilian immigrants in Boston, Martes (1999), based on a survey of 300 Brazilian immigrants and 40 informal interviews, found the sample to be mainly from the Brazilian lower middle class with a secondary school education, a level similar to Hispanics in the U.S. The social class and educational differences of Brazilians in Boston from that of Brazilians in New York indicated by Margolis (1994) are once more confirmed. In Marte's study most of the sample was married and lived with their children in the U.S. A great proportion of the Brazilians in Boston used to work in the service sector in Brazil. In the U.S. the service sector was also an area of concentration, especially housecleaning. Margolis (1994) states that the job market for household workers in New York and elsewhere in the U.S. has greatly increased in recent years as the former full-time, housewife-mother entered the job market to sustain a middle-class standard of living. Based on her research findings, Martes (2000) argues that ethnicity does not guarantee solidarity among ethnic social networks. According to her, the exchange of housecleaning contracts among immigrants illustrates the conflict and ambiguity in relationships among immigrants. The exchange consist in selling to another immigrant the contact of houses to be cleaned when one does not intend to continue in housecleaning either because she/he is going back to Brazil or starting another type of work. Thus, the new housecleaner pays an amount to be referred by the previous one to the house residents. Established Brazilian immigrants "capitalize their business by spinning off homes to new arrivals"(Millman 1997, p.232).

Reasons for Immigrating

Social scientists explain international migration by two main approaches: the push-pull model, a more traditional view that proposes an imbalance in labor supply and labor demand as the cause for international migration; and the structural model that proposes macroeconomic trade and investment flows between the countries as the catalysts for international migration. While proponents of the push-pull model emphasize individual responses, structuralists emphasize the global scenario. Margolis (1994) argues that both approaches are not mutually exclusive, but useful when considering different levels of analysis. Brazil, as one of the new industrializing nations, has entered the cycle of transnational migration in the industrialized world. As Margolis (1994) suggests in the preface of her book:

> The benefits of transnational migration to the industrialized world are substantial: it channels in a

mass of low-cost, often well educated workers, who are willing, even eager, to take a variety of jobs that otherwise might go unfilled. And at the same time, it relieves some of the economic and political pressures that might otherwise threaten the stability of numerous newly industrializing nations. It is well to keep these global issues in mind when looking at particular migrant flows to particular countries (p.xvii).

Portes (1990) explains that the underlying assumptions of the "push" and "pull" model are that the most disadvantaged members of poorer societies migrate in search of labor and that flows arise spontaneously due to the economic inequalities worldwide. However, empirical reality attests that major flows frequently originate in countries at intermediate levels of development and were, "each in its time, subjects of expansionist pattern through which successive U.S. governments sought to remold the country's immediate periphery"(p.225).

At the individual level it might be said that the push factors for Brazilians to leave the country are linked to economics. In fact, the emigration floodgates opened at the time that the Cruzado Plan, the government's attempt to control inflation, failed in 1986. Brazil at that time was faced with the saying "it has to work," but it did not. "The new generation gets desperate with the lack of opportunities in Brazil and searches for alternatives" ("O povo da diaspora", 8/7/91). Moreover, many middle-class professionals in Brazil were either unable to find a job in the field of their training or even if employed, received salaries so low they were forced to hold two or three jobs in order to meet their needs. A middle-class standard of living was, and continues to be, increasingly difficult to sustain.

The search for a better future for the next generation constitutes another motivational factor linked to economics. Brazilians no longer see the possibility of providing good quality education for their children in their own country. A good education means having one's children in private schools, which present higher costs each year ("Aumenta exodo", 11/4/90). These circumstances continue to apply.

In terms of pull factors, Massachusetts originally attracted Brazilian immigrants with stories of its economic boom during the mid-1980s (Franklin, 2/3/92). Even after the economic recession of the early 90s, Brazilians concentrated on self-employment and found the housecleaning business recession proof (Millman, 1997). But other, non-economic factors also attracted immigrants. According to the Immigration and Naturalization Service in Boston, many Brazilians came to Massachusetts because of its large Portuguese-speaking population (Coleman, 10/8/89) made up of earlier immigrants from Portugal, the Cape Verde Islands, and the Azores.

Portes (1990) points out that migration involves a social network. He proposes an alternative approach stressing the microstructures of labor migration. As he explains, socially embedded migration explains the predisposition to move and the enduring character of migration flows. Therefore, social networks constitute a major determinant of the ties between sending and receiving places of migration: "More than a movement that follows automatically the push and pull of economic conditions, labor migration should be conceptualized as a process of progressive network building"(p.232).

In fact, social networks and the established Brazilian community in Boston are essential factors in the continuous arrival of newcomers. In the greater Boston area

Cambridge, Allston-Brighton, East Boston, Somerville, Framingham and Marlborough are towns with significant Brazilian populations (Martes, 1998). In these towns, bilingual Portuguese-English programs are offered in the public schools and there is a concentration of ethnic stores, restaurants and other services with Portuguese-speaking employees. Such trends are shown in a newspaper article reporting the installation by one of the town's oldest financial institutions of a trilingual English-Portuguese-Spanish automated-teller machine in Framingham's downtown (Vigue, 02/19/95). The Massachusetts Alliance of Portuguese Speakers, reports that the Portuguese-speaking community is the fourth largest ethnic group in the state (Nguyen, 08/06/95).

Moreover, Brazilians have their own newspapers such as the *Brazilian Times*, a weekly tabloid with a circulation of 25,000, and eleven other newspapers and two monthly magazines in Boston, all in Portuguese (Greenhalgh, 1999; Salgado & Carelli, 2001). Since August 1999 Brazilians have been able to watch a Brazilian television channel. The cable channel TV Globo, the most powerful television producer in Brazil, is available through subscription (Greenhalgh, 1999) and has already thirty thousand subscribers in the U.S. (Salgado & Carelli, 2001). On that channel, Brazilians can watch soap operas, news, football games and other Brazilian programs. Brazilians also have religious and community programs on cable TV such as the "Jovem Cristão" or Christian Youth, a show produced by a local Brazilian evangelical church in Portuguese (Tomlinson, 2001). Further, the Internet has been a valuable source of exchange of information to Brazilians. The Brazilian consulate's web site provides information on support services that help Brazilians abroad maintain a social network. Thus, on the consulate's home page one may access information such as: the Brazilian citizens council, Brazilian cultural events in the New England area, a list of lawyers, a list of health care and social services professionals who are either Brazilian or speak Portuguese, information on science and technology, information about Brazil and the Brazilian business network. This way, anyone can contact the Brazilian organizations that provide services to Brazilians living in the U.S. There are about eight or ten Brazilian organizations (Sales, 1999) in Massachusetts. They were created in the early and mid 90s with various goals: the Brazilian Immigrant Center, founded in 1995, helps immigrants on labor issues; the Brazilian Community Center, linked to the First Brazilian Baptist Church, assists immigrants; the Brazilian Professional Network promotes meetings of interest to immigrants with businesses; the Massachusetts Alliance of Portuguese Speakers provides health (including mental health) and social services; the Brazilian Women's Group has a discussion group and promotes cultural events. Recently, on the Internet an on-line newspaper has been created specifically for Brazilians living in the U.S., "Aldeialink" offers recent news about Brazil. The articles usually include thoughts on being an immigrant or from an immigrant's point of view, and a list of bilingual Portuguese-English jobs around the U.S.

The significant role social network play on migration is shown in a study by the Center of Immigrant Studies in New York. According to their results, more than 52% of Brazilians that immigrate to the U.S. already have friends with whom to stay with when they first arrive and in 25% of the cases they come with the intention to stay permanently. In less than 20 days, 65% of Brazilian immigrants get a job, a fact attesting to an established community network (Canzian, 07/11/94).

CHAPTER 2
Acculturation

The concept of culture has been widely studied in the anthropological field and has been a frequently used concept in cross-cultural psychological research as well as a theme of study in culturally aware clinical practice and research. As Rohner (1984) in an examination of the concept of culture explains, within anthropology there seems to be two broad and somewhat opposing views on the nature of culture. The boundaries between these two views, however, are often blurry since each introduces significant elements of the other into ones discussions. There are those who consider culture as behavior, organized modes of behavior in familial, political, religious, technological and other institutional domains in a society. Others understand culture as a system of symbols, an ideational system, a system of meanings in the minds of multiple individuals in a population. Within the so called ideational theories Rohner identifies three approaches, one based on the linguistic model in the sense that cultures would be epistemologically in the same realm as languages, behind the realm of observable events there are inferred ideational codes; a second view is the structuralist approach; and a third is the one that views culture as a symbolic system. In the symbolic system approach, Rohner defines culture as "the totality of equivalent and complementary learned meanings maintained by a human population, or by identifiable segments of a population, and transmitted from one generation to the next"(p.120). Moreover as Geertz (1988) says: "Believing, with Max Weber, that man is an animal suspended in webs of significance he himself has spun, I take culture to be those webs, and the analysis of it to be therefore not an experimental science in search of law but an interpretative one in search of meaning".

In spite of conceptual differences, culture theorists argue that culture refers to a learned phenomenon reflecting an orderliness and regularity of human life, an organized whole, and varies greatly from one population to another. Basically, it refers to the way of life of a people that in some way is shared (Rohner, 1984). Falicov (1995), advocating a multi-dimensional perspective in family therapy, also defines culture as "sets of shared world views, meanings and adaptive behaviors derived from simultaneous membership and participation in a multiplicity of contexts, such as rural, urban or suburban setting; language, age, gender, cohort, family configuration, race, ethnicity, religion, nationality, socioeconomic status, employment, education, occupation, sexual orientation, political ideology; migration and stage of acculturation" (p.375). Further, Rohner affirms that although culture is not behavior, many investigators who do cultural analyses depend on behavior as the major source of data. He cites Geertz who sustains that it is through the flow of behavior, that is, social action, that cultural forms find articulation.

When two distinct cultural groups come in continuous contact, a process of cultural change or acculturation results

(Berry, Kim, Mind & Mok, 1987; Berry, Poortinga, Segal & Dasen, 1992; Danzinger, 1974; Mena, Padilla, & Maldonado, 1987; Padilla, Wagatsuma, & Lindholm, 1985; Phinney, Chavira, & Williamson, 1992). Both groups may change through this process. Nonetheless, in one of his studies, Berry (1980) explains that though in principle change could occur in either of the two groups, in reality one group dominates the other, leading to a distinction between the "dominant group" and the "acculturating group." Yet, as Berry et al. (1992) say, this does not mean that changes in the dominant culture are unimportant since acculturation implies among other things population expansion, cultural diversification, attitudinal reactions such as prejudice and discrimination, and policy development involving cultural pluralism, bilingual schooling and related phenomena.

Most studies of acculturation focus on the adjustment of newcomers. Some scholars have extended the definition of acculturation from a group level phenomenon to an individual level phenomenon (Berry et al., 1987). Thus, acculturation may be considered as a two-level phenomenon: that of the group and that of the individual. Psychological acculturation refers to the psychological changes that occur to an individual whose cultural group is collectively culturally changing. In this sense, acculturation is an adaptive experience (Mena et al., 1987; Padilla et al., 1985). The distinction between the group level and individual level acculturation is important for two reasons. One is that the phenomena are different in each level, affecting distinct aspects: changes in social structure, economic base, and political organization generally occur at the population level, while at the individual level changes in identity, values, and attitudes are common. Further the participation of the acculturating individuals in the collective changes are not in the same way (Berry et < biblio >). By cultural change it is understood that the immigrant's beliefs, values and customs gradually undergo a transformation through which the individual supposedly adapts to the new environment.

This adjustment process is conceived in two distinct ways with respect to how the immigrant group's cultural adaptation is considered in relation to the dominant culture. As Phinney explains (1990), a linear, bipolar model assumes that as the immigrant becomes immersed in the mainstream society, acculturation necessarily means that the customs and values of the majority culture replace those of the cultures of origin, or in other words, the dominant culture must be adopted. This linear model (a traditional one, at least as it is applied in the United States) assumes that as people take on the values, customs and language of a new culture, they drop the values, customs and language of their old culture (Azar, 1999).

In contrast, a two-dimensional process model considers concomitantly not only the immigrant's relation to the predominant culture but also to his or her culture of origin. Thus, adaptation to the new environment is multi-dimensional; it occurs at least in two directions, i.e., biculturally, although not necessarily at the same rate in both directions (Cuellar, Harris, and Jasso, 1980).

From a bicultural perspective, one can acculturate in many different ways. Therefore, theoretical and empirical formulations need to describe and measure the degree of acquisition of the customs of a new society as well as the degree of retention of native cultural customs. Berry (1980) suggests varieties of adaptation that can be approached by considering the relation of the individual to his/her own culture and to the dominant culture. The ways in which a group or acculturating individual relates to the dominant society are known as acculturation strategies. These central issues generate a conceptual framework that considers whether the individual or group value maintaining their cultural identity and characteristics and/or establishing relationships and maintaining characteristics and values of the host society.

Although in reality these issues can be responded to in an attitudinal continuum, a dichotomous response (yes or no) for the purpose of conceptual presentation is formulated. In this respect, four varieties of acculturation appear: deculturation, rejection, integration and assimilation. Sub-categories are based on whether the dominant society permitted the individual any choice in cultural orientation.

A negative relation to the host culture forms two modes of acculturation: 1) Deculturation, non-identification with either the major or one's own culture, and 2) Rejection, opposition to a positive relationship with the main society but maintenance of a cultural identity. Deculturalization results in the marginalization of a group when it resists change or in ethnocide when the resistance comes from the dominant society. Rejection may exist in the form of withdrawal or segregation in response to the larger society.

Two other responses demonstrate an acceptance of the dominant society's culture but vary in the value they place on retaining the original cultural identity: 3) Integration, maintenance of cultural identity concomitant with an effort to join the dominant society, and 4) Assimilation, a renunciation of cultural identity and movement into the larger society. In assimilation the major society may be either plural or multicultural. Plural societies gather a diversity of cultural groups but in multicultural societies the diversity of the groups is valued. Subvarieties of these categories occur when the larger society permits the group to move freely, the "Melting Pot," or alternatively, when the groups are forced into mainstream society, the "Pressure Cooker".

Similarly, Mendoza and Martinez (1981) describe four typological patterns of acculturation. The first is cultural resistance, consisting of an active or passive opposition to dominant cultural norms while maintaining original customs. The second is cultural shift, which occurs whenever there is a substitution of one set of practices by alternate cultural characteristics, as exhibited by simultaneous assimilation and extinction. The third is cultural incorporation, when there is adaptation of patterns from both cultural groups: assimilation without extinction. Finally, the fourth is cultural transmutation, an alteration of certain elements of both cultures to create a third, somewhat unique, subcultural entity. Besides these, researchers suggest a modality dimension, comprised of cognitive, affective and behavioral aspects of the individual experiencing acculturation. Thus, with the exposure to the new environment transformations may occur in regard to beliefs, attitudes, behaviors and feelings grounded in one's previous cultural setting.

Padilla (1980) views acculturation as a multidimensional model based on two elements: cultural awareness and ethnic loyalty. Cultural awareness refers to the individual's knowledge of specific cultural aspects such as language, values, foods and other characteristics of both the culture of origin and the host culture, including the degree of inter-ethnic interaction. Ethnic loyalty regards the preference for one cultural orientation over the other, that is, the inclination the individual has toward either the original or the adopted culture, perceived discrimination, and social behavior orientation. Such dimensions constitute the parameters from which Padilla derives a typology of acculturation and relates them to other variables such as generation, education, language preference and use in a multidimensional model.

Thus, theoretical models of acculturation clearly show that this adjustment process is mediated by many different factors. Some models present overlapping variables, others emphasize different areas of the cultural adaptation process. Berry et al. (1987) and Dyal (1981) have pointed out specific conditions under which immigration occurs and some specific characteristics of the acculturating group which predict cultural adaptation.

A crucial characteristic is the degree to which the host society provides opportunity for social, economic and occupational mobility. Another is government policy and informal social structures based on a multicultural pluralistic philosophy of inter-group relations or on an assimilationist melting pot ideology. Not only are the host society's attitudes toward immigrants a factor but so is the support networks available to the immigrant. For instance, as Berry et al (1992) explain, in Canada, an immigrant receiving country, early policies favored assimilation. Later in 1971, seeing that assimilation had not worked in any other country and was impractical, the Canadian government announced a national multiculturalism policy in order to break discriminatory attitudes and cultural jealousies. This policy encourages self-confidence by supporting the various cultures and ethnic groups that are understood to enrich the society. In contrast to culturally monistic societies, plural societies offer a network of social and cultural groups that may provide support for the newcomers and greater tolerance and acceptance of cultural diversity. Thus, government policies are intrinsically linked to how immigrants are accepted or not in the new country, and consequently, they affect the immigrant's adjustment. In the U.S., as Suárez-Orozco and Suárez-Orozco (1995) indicated, Proposition 187 in California, which, among other measures, excluded undocumented immigrant children from elementary and secondary schools, is paradigmatic of an anti-immigrant climate, in which immigrants are seen as people taking advantage of American benefits. The authors argue that the phenomenon is by no means limited to California or to the U.S. but is a global issue for over 100 million immigrants worldwide.

However, there are lower rates of health problems among immigrants in pluralistic societies accepting a diversity of cultures in contrast to assimilationist ones requiring that the mainstream culture be assumed by all. Research has shown, for instance, that Canada differs substantially from the US and Australia in the ratio of mental health problems. Having controlled for age, ethnicity and other demographic factors, researchers found that in Canada immigrants were less at risk of mental health problems than non-immigrants while immigrants in the U.S. and Australia were at greater risk than non-immigrants. These findings seem to be related to the different implicit intergroup ideologies operating in the three countries (Dyal and Dyal, 1980). Such findings might be related in some respect to the study by Goza (1994) mentioned in the first chapter, in which Goza shows that significantly more Brazilian immigrants in Canada wanted to reside permanently in that country and improve their English skills in contrast to the Brazilians in the U.S. who wanted to return to Brazil.

Regarding the acculturating group's characteristics, demographic features like gender, age, generation, social class, marital status, education, and legal status are important to adaptation. For instance, Mena et. al. (1987) compared immigration age in a systematic way and found that the age of 12 was the decisive for determining high levels of stress among immigrants. Accordingly immigrants may be described as early immigrants if they immigrated before the age of 12 or late immigrants when immigration occurred after that age. Padilla et al. (1985) found that late immigrants and second generation subjects experienced the most stress compared to early immigrants and third generation individuals. The second generation is literally caught between two cultures, that of their parents and that of the larger society. Regarding social class, immigration can often mean downward mobility when a negative change in socioeconomic status occurs. Whereas upward mobility may be reassuring and reinforce feelings of control, a change to lower status with underemployment or unemployment are factors that increase the difficulty of adjusting to the new society (Woon, 1996).

However, Mendoza (1989) suggests that acculturation instruments based only on demographic factors fail to detect the variability of acculturation within immigrant groups, and should be restricted to a support for the validity of instruments based on actual indicators of cultural customs.

Further, the immigrants' motivation and level of participation in the migration process are factors that furnish information about the individual's disposition towards the new cultural environment. The newcomer's dominant motivations may be economic, political, personal and familial. As Mendoza and Martinez (1981) indicate, an individual who leaves the country of origin out of dissatisfaction and with no intention of returning would probably have different attitudes toward the cultural customs of the receiving society than would an individual who left out of economic necessity and had strong desires to return. In addition, the level of participation in the decision to migrate may not be equal among family members (Shuval, 1993). In traditional marriages the wives tend to be less active in the decision-making process. This level of participation will affect the subsequent process of adjustment to the new environment. Other factors studied have been personal traits such as self-esteem and locus of control, also relevant factors in the adaptation process (Mena et al., 1987; Padilla et. a., 1985).

Therefore, research studies need to take into account the complexity of acculturation. It cannot be measured with a single variable such as language. Mendoza (1989) suggests that multiple items that sample and measure relatively orthogonal dimensions of acculturation need to be incorporated. For instance, one can be cognitively bicultural by speaking both English and another language and display affective cultural shift by having attitudes that reflect the majority culture, but have concomitant food preferences and habits that are different from those of the mainstream society.

Berry (1980) suggested three typical stages during the development of acculturation: contact, conflict and adaptation. The first phase is essential, the second likely, and some form of the third unavoidable. The nature, objective and duration of the contact affect the acculturation process. Some degree of resistance to the dominant culture occurs since groups do not easily give up valued features of their culture. Thus, conflict at some point seems likely, whereas adaptation comes as a phase in which through a variety of ways conflict is reduced or stabilized.

Conflict implies some degree of stress whereas adaptation presupposes coping.

Acculturative stress is a specific kind of stress in which the stressors are often culture-specific. Thus, to qualify as acculturative stress, the stress behaviors that effect the health of individuals, including physical, psychological and social factors, should be related in a systematic way to known features of the acculturation process, such as the ones mentioned above, as experienced by the individual (Berry at al., 1992). Individuals participate and experience changes in acculturation to varying degrees, leading to varying levels of acculturative stress. The researchers affirm that the relationships among these three concepts, acculturation experience, stressors and acculturative stress, depend on a number of moderating factors including the mode (or acculturation strategies as described above) and phase of acculturation, the nature of the larger society, the type of acculturating group, and the demographic, social, and psychological characteristics of the group and its individual members. While an earlier view of acculturative stress was that cultural contact and change inevitably led to stress, current views are that stress is linked to acculturation and the level of stress experienced depends on various factors. One key factor is coping: some scholars maintain that for a stressed individual to function satisfactorily, a process of coping with the difficult circumstances has to occur for adaptation to be achieved (Berry et al., 1987; Mena et al., 1987). Coping is defined by Mena et al. as a cognitive response that reduces or removes the negative effects of stress. Coping mechanisms may involve psychological resources, social resources and specific coping resources. Psychological resources refer to personality characteristics such as locus of control, strong commitment to oneself, and the perception of life changes as challenges rather than threats. Social resources include support from family and friends. The study suggested that specific coping resources among the sample "were either to take an active, planned action to reduce stress or just to talk with others about the problem" (p. 221). Further, the study also showed that locus of control constitutes a predictor of acculturative stress for all generations of immigrants.

Grinberg and Grinberg (1989), from a psychoanalytical perspective, consider that the adaptation of the migrant to the new environment depends on the interplay of emotional attitudes and reactions of both the emigrant and the people of the host environment and the quality of attachment that develops between them. The authors understand that the attachment established depends on the type of object relations the individual had before emigrating and by the object relations of the host community, assuming that this can be understood at the group level. The authors aim to systematize a psychopathology of migration and understand migration as a crisis or traumatic situation. As they explain "... we would suggest that migration is a potentially traumatic experience characterized by a series of partially traumatic events and at the same time represents a crisis situation" (p. 15). The prototype of migratory experience would be the trauma of birth and the loss of the protective mother. In this perspective of the emotional internal world, migration can arouse different anxieties: persecutory anxieties in response to change, the new and the unknown; depressive anxieties leading to mourning of the objects left behind and the lost parts of the self, and disorienting anxieties due to the failure to distinguish between the old

Acculturation

and the new. These anxieties, symptoms and defense mechanisms are part of the psychopathology of migration. Thus, migration puts the individual's psychic and emotional stability to the test. A person must have a good relation to internal objects, accept the losses and work through the mourning process to be able to integrate the two countries, time periods and social groups in a discriminating way.

Sluski (1997), focusing on the effects of disruption and reconstruction of social networks in migration, argues that the interpersonal, psychosomatic and somatic problems the loss of social support brings are a natural consequence of the move, in an increasingly mobile world. Paradoxically at the same time that the move to a new country increases the migrant's need for social support, it represents a rupture of previous social links. This natural disturbance brings more stress to family members and the family dynamics, since each might expect from other family members what was before satisfied by extra family connections.

In an earlier study, based on clinical experience and workshops, Sluski (1979) described five stages that families undergo during the migration process:

1) The preparatory stage. The time span varies according to family style, which may be the result of an explosive decision or of lengthy rumination. Motivations may have positive or negative connotations, but even a positive motivation, seeking a better living, implies something negative, escaping from a bad living situation. Such motives underlie the family's future style of coping. A common consequence is the scapegoating of a family member. If the move had a positive motivation and things go well, there is no reason for mourning. The member in charge of mourning has a chance of being

scapegoated. The opposite may also occur. Families remaining attached to their past--in a state of mourning--may consider the first member to break away from this atmosphere a traitor.

2) The act of migration. Styles of migration vary. Some families burn bridges and migration is something definite; others believe in a temporary arrangement even though return is unlikely.

3) Overcompensation. The immigrants are generally unaware of the stressful nature of migration, and following the move, the families focus on survival. Family disorganization may occur, but generally there is a moratorium, which can be sustained by the belief in a return to the country of origin after some time.

4) Decompensation or crisis. After the moratorium the family's previous values may prove ineffective in the new country. A division of roles may occur as a coping device. One member, usually the male, deals with present-future activities in the new environment, while another member, usually the woman, maintains connections with the previous country. However, such rigidity escalates to a crisis in the relationship. Another common conflict is when women acquire a new role by beginning work, challenging family male-dominated structure.

5) Transgenerational impact. Whatever was avoided in the first generation will be expressed in the second, creating conflicts between generations.

Further, as Sales (1984) points out, adjustment is a process that proceeds with time. The more time an immigrant spends in the new country, the fewer difficulties he or she will experience in everyday life. In addition, with time one tends to stereotype the new culture less and perceive the complexity of the new society.

However, as noted above acculturation transcends the newcomers' process and constitutes a dynamic intergenerational process (Sluski, 1979; Suarez-Orozco & Suarez-Orozco, 1995).

CHAPTER 3
Gender Roles

Gender roles or sex roles are an individual's endorsement of personal characteristics, occupations and behaviors considered appropriate for women and men in a particular culture. As Fowlkes (1987) points out, the concept of role allows us to see the links between the individual, the social order and the culture. Roles constitute a patterned cluster of behaviors and attitudes that are culturally prescribed. Individuals act and interact according to these prescribed understandings of what is appropriate and expected of them. In regard to gender roles, individuals will behave and interact in ways that conform to a constellation of qualities understood to characterize males and females in their culture. As Block asserts, "The development of sex role identity is influenced by both biological and historical-cultural factors in complex interaction and with changing degrees of ascendancy at different critical periods" (p. 513).

Psychoanalysts such as Nancy Chodorow (1974, 1978) and Jean Baker Miller (1986) understand women and men's gender role formation as being embedded in a socio-cultural context and question the "anatomy is destiny" postulation of Freudian theory. Thus, Chodorow attributes sex differences not to anatomy but to the fact that women, universally, are largely responsible for early childcare. Her theory posits that sex differences in personality are fundamentally a result of this early social environment that is experienced differently by male and female children. Mothers tend to experience daughters as more like and continuous with themselves and sons as their male opposites. Thus, girls' identity formation is a fusing experience of attachment to the mother, whereas for boys, identifying themselves as males separate from their mothers curtails their primary love and sense of empathic tie. Consequently male gender identity is threatened by intimacy while female gender identity is threatened by separation.

Miller uses psychoanalytic concepts to analyze women's subordinate position in society, addressing the inequality of power and authority between men and women to understand how it shapes female experience and personality. Women are treated and believed to be men's subordinates and are ascribed the psychological characteristics of subordinates such as submissiveness, passivity, docility, dependency, lack of initiative, and the like. Subordinates know much more about the dominants than vice-versa since they need to be highly attuned to the dominants. As Miller explains, that is the origin of the commonly mentioned feminine intuition and feminine wiles. A female belief in a male magical strength, which enables them to manage in the outside world and thus provide for the family, coexists side by side with an intimate knowledge of his weakness. The author states that the expression of "penis envy" is actually a simple explanation for women's lack of access to the real world. If the woman accepts the male conception of females she will not be conscious of a conflict of interests or needs, but assume that her needs are fulfilled if she is oriented around the primacy of men and service to their needs. Thus, male and female children are raised believing in male superiority and the subservience of women.

Thus, gender perspectives help us to understand human behavior as emerging from a constellation of interactions between women and men as biological beings and their social environment. Biologically males and females have different sex organs and sex hormones to which collective images that include values, cultural beliefs (stereotypes), and expectations (ideology) are transposed. This leads to sex differences in child rearing, role differentiation assignment and sex differences in various psychological characteristics such as aggression, abilities and the like (Berry, Poortinga, Segall & Dasen, 1992). Human behavior is framed by a gendered social environment and cannot be a biologically-sex-determined behavior devoid of social context (Gilbert, 1993).

Gender roles: A historical view

Gender roles are not static and change as the needs of society change. A historical view demonstrates this point. Sociologists, historians, anthropologists and psychologists describe the changes that women's roles have undergone (Chafetz and Hagan, 1996; Luepnitz, 1988; Margolis, 1984). During the eighteenth and nineteenth century there was a change in the ideology of motherhood. The importance of a close mother-child bond appears in the French Enlightenment, particularly in the work of Jean-Jacques Rousseau which coincided with an interest in increasing the French population for political reasons. Further, the rise of capitalism during the eighteenth and nineteenth centuries meant a shift in the family from a unit of production to a unit of consumption. Thus, home and work, which were once the same place, became split into two different spheres. As Luepnitz explains, those changes for the rising middle class meant a sharp division of the world according to gender. Thus female economic dependence and constitution of home as a feminine sphere are fairly recent artifacts of industrialization in western society (Margolis, 1984).

In the United States, the isolation of the urban middle class woman began with industrialization when men went to work in factories becoming the sole family breadwinners (Walker & Wallston, 1985). Later in the 1950s women who had held jobs during World War II because men were at war were expected to vacate them after the war ended and return to their pre-war housewife status. Margolis speaks of the 1950s as a time when women must have suffered from cognitive dissonance. There was a contrast between a large number of married women in the labor force and the advice of childcare experts and the popular media who praised the feminine mystique and advocated their supposedly right place at home.

A transition period began in the 1960's when the contradiction of reality and ideology started to be challenged. In 1963 Betty Friedan's *The Feminine Mystique* was published. Further, in the 1970's an increasing number of working class families were unable to live on the husband's wages alone due to a decline in family income (Hood, 1986; Scarr, Phillips, McCartney, 1989). During the 70s questioning of the posited mother role became common. Feminist ideology in the late 60s and 70s induced a revision of past theories, denouncing the contrast between what women were experiencing and the theories based on patriarchal values.

Gender roles: Division of labor

Women's increased participation in the labor force made the reality of dual-earner families a common scenario. Household labor division became an important matter for the family and was observed by social scientists. The reality of women's life within the home was not a fairy tale as depicted in many 50s movies. Women, besides working outside of the home, were still doing most of the household tasks. Studies done on time spent on household work flourished in the 1960s beginning with the publication of Blood and Wolfe's (1960) *Husbands and Wives* (Perry-Jenkins & Crouter, 1990; Pleck ,1985). The researchers proposed what came to be known as resource theory. The basic tenet assumed that the couple balanced work inside the home according to their respective resources brought from outside. They concluded that husbands whose wives were employed were more involved with home duties. The other two dominant theories in family studies to address the division of labor were Scanzoni's (1970) "Exchange Theory" and Parson and Bales' (1955) classic formulation of role differentiation. The exchange theory postulates that each partner's contribution to the mutual exchange performance within the family places an obligation on the other partner to provide his/her reciprocal contribution. For instance, husbands exchange their successful performance in the family breadwinner role for their wives' provision of love, companionship, household services and childcare. On the other hand, the role differentiation theory posited that women and men have distinct roles in family. The male role is an instrumental one with responsibility for the family's relation to the outside world, essentially through his job, and the female role is an expressive one with responsibility for dealing with the family's internal needs.

In the 1970's, large scale surveys on time use allowed researchers to describe how much work husbands and wives did in absolute terms. Their findings contradicted the traditional theoretical perspective applied to dual earner couples, indicating that husbands of employed wives did not perform more housework and childcare than did husbands of full-time homemakers. As Pleck (1985) says "In light of these data, it became intellectually untenable to view the husband's limited family role as the result of an equitable exchange between husband and wife based on their having different resources" (p.15). It was shown that employed wives experienced role overload. Feminist critique of the unequal family division of labor resulting from a norm of male intellectual and occupational achievement superiority was compatible with the results of the time use studies.

The focus of the studies during the 1980s were on the reasons for women's double work and men's inequitable participation (Coleman, 1988; Denmark, Shaw and Ciali, 1985; Hochschild, 1989; O'Leary, Unger and Wallston, 1985). Gender role ideology or gender role attitude was indicated as a major determinant of the division of family work.

Gender Role Attitudes

Gender role attitudes or gender role ideology constitute the acceptance of cultural beliefs about how women and men should behave. As Winstead and Derlega (1993) indicate, women and men's behaviors in close relationships are influenced by their acceptance of cultural beliefs on how each sex should behave. Two basic themes are central to traditional sex role ideology. One theme emphasizes a gender-based division of labor. Traditionally homemaking and childcare have been defined as women's work and paid employment as men's work. The other theme is male dominance, commonly reflected in the belief that the husband should be the head of the family and should take the lead in making decisions. Peplau, Hill and Rubin (1993) conceptualize sex role attitudes as varying along a continuum, from strict adherence to traditional norms to a rejection of old norms in favor of principles of equality.

In an in depth study of couples' life arrangements regarding family work, Hoschild (1989) found that deep gender ideology permeated the relation of husbands and wives. She suggests that each individual adopts a gender strategy in which ideology is reconciled with his or her own behavior. The individual's gender ideology determines what sphere he/she wants to identify with (home or work) and how much power in the marriage he/she wants to have. Hochschild identifies three types of ideology of marital roles: a) pure traditional - the woman wants to identify with her activities at home while her husband is concerned with work; she wants less power than him and the man agrees; b) pure egalitarian - some couples might want to be jointly oriented to the home, others to their careers, or both of them to jointly hold some balance between the two; c) transitional - a typical transitional woman wants to identify both with caring for the home and helping her husband earn money but wants her husband to focus on earning a living. A typical transitional man is in favor of his wife working but wants her to take the main responsibility at home. The relationship between gender role attitudes and behavior such as division of household tasks seems to be a complex one.

Many studies on gender roles refer to traditional versus modern or liberal gender roles. Traditional sex-roles encompass the assumption that the only significant role for women is taking care of the home and children while the men work and provide financially for the family (Behrman, 1982). This view emphasizes characteristics for each sex that are related to these distinct spheres of life. Thus, independence, individuality and self-reliance for males and connectedness, nurturance and emotional expressivity for females are emphasized (Gilligan, 1982; Miller, 1976; Peplau and Gordon, 1985; Pleck, 1976). Moreover, males' interpersonal and emotional skills are relatively underdeveloped and feelings of tenderness and vulnerability are forbidden whereas females are encouraged to develop such skills and feelings.

In contrast, more liberal gender roles refer to an equal sharing of financial and domestic responsibilities between males and females and encouragement of the development of women's talents and careers (Behrman, 1982). Thus, interpersonal skills which promote collaboration with others is expected for males (Pleck, 1976) and self-determination and self-reliance are expected for females (Miller, 1976). In other words, people who are more liberal will behave, feel and have attitudes that were traditionally regarded as norms for the opposite sex. Traditional gender roles affect individuals of both sexes in various aspects of their lives such as how they communicate, how they structure their networks of support, how they divide family work, as well as how they think and feel about women and men in traditional and nontraditional roles. Studies have shown that even emotions such as fear are related to men's and women's gender role behaviors and occupations (Brody, 1993).

The fundamental themes in the male role stress achievement and suppress affect. In the traditional male role the major forms of achievement that validate masculinity are physical. Interpersonal and emotional skills are relatively undeveloped, and feelings of tenderness and vulnerability are especially prohibited as indicated by Brody (1993). Anger and impulsive behavior are encouraged, especially with other males, and are often experienced as particularly validating of masculinity. Pleck (1976) maintains that the traditional male expects women to acknowledge and defer to his authority. Marital relationships are viewed as primarily functional; the contemporary concept of intimacy does not take place; and men's relationships with other females are kept at a minimum. The traditional male role prescribes that men have strong emotional bonds to other men. Those relationships often take ritualized forms that limit intimacy, although they are important and usually stronger than men's ties to women.

In contrast, Pleck (1976) explains that achievement in the modern male role takes other forms, requiring more interpersonal and intellectual skills than physical strength. Interpersonal skills are expected, especially insofar as these promote smooth collaboration with others toward achievement, as in management. Capacity for tenderness and emotional intimacy are also encouraged, but closely restricted to romantic heterosexual relationships and excluded elsewhere. Staying emotionally "cool" is a major value, and anger and impulsive behavior are particularly prohibited. The more modern male expects companionship and intimacy in his marital relationship. Heterosexual relationships are seen as the only source of legitimate emotional support needed in the daily struggle. In contrast to the traditional male, the modern male does not expect his female companion to defer to his authority, but that she soothe his wounds and replenish his emotional reserves, which places different, but equally limiting demands on women. Emotional relationships with other men are weak and generally absent, though a high level of competence in conducting work relationships is expected. The modern male discloses more to other females than to other male friends. Compared to the traditional role, the relation with other men and not with other women seems pragmatic and functional.

Despite the connection between gender role attitudes and behavior, studies indicate that becoming more liberal does not necessarily mean that the men will share household chores. Brody and Flanagan (1990) found that household tasks did not vary as a function of changes in gender role attitudes for men.

Gender roles and marital satisfaction

Research has analyzed the relationships among components of gender roles, such as personality attributes, attitudes towards gender roles, division of household tasks, and marital satisfaction. Most studies address personality traits such as masculinity, femininity and androgynous characteristics in relation to marital satisfaction (Campbell & Snow, 1992; Cooper, Chassin, Braver, Zeiss & Khavari, 1986; Juni & Grimm, 1993; Zammichieli, Gilroy & Sherman, 1988). In general, an increase in the husband's femininity, being more expressive and nurturant, is related to an increase in his wife's in marital satisfaction (Campbell & Snow, 1992) as well as his own (Cooper et. al., 1986; Juni & Grimm, 1993). Other studies indicated that when both partners were androgynous marital satisfaction was higher (Zammichieli et al., 1988).

Gender Roles

The relationship between gender role attitudes and marital quality has been examined by some studies. It has been suggested that similar attitudes are related to greater marital satisfaction (Gilbert, 1985). Supporting this idea, Bowen and Orthner (1983) found that when the husband was traditional and the wife modern the marriage had the lowest evaluation. However, when the husband was modern and the wife traditional and when spouses had congruent sex role attitudes, satisfaction in marriage was similar, both being higher. Lye and Biblarz (1993) found that couples with similar attitudes have higher levels of marital satisfaction than couples who disagree. Similar to other research findings, the results indicate that when men are less traditional than their wives, overall disagreements are reduced but when women are less traditional then their husbands overall disagreements are increased.

Studies have indicated the greater importance of household labor division in comparison to demographic variables in explaining marital satisfaction (Suitor, 1988). Beinin and Agostinelli (1988) found that the way total work hours are distributed between spouses determines satisfaction in the marital relationship. Wives' satisfaction with the division of labor increased with the participation of husbands in more traditional feminine tasks. Hochschild (1990) found that couples in which the husband performed more household and childcare duties were happier. The men who shared more household work were more satisfied with their family life. In their involvement with childcare they were performing a pattern of parenthood that differed from their own fathers.

Discrepancies between gender role attitudes and behavior between spouses have been reported in greater extent in problematic marriages in which couples were either separating or in counseling than in non-problem marriages (Gilbert, 1985).

Gender roles in Brazilian society: A historical view

Brazil's current gender roles trace back to the historical origins of the Brazilian family, with the Portuguese colonizers who established a patriarchal organization consisting of extended kinship, traditional gender roles and childrearing (Candido, 1951; Freyre, 1964; Pierson, 1954; Sa, 1947; Wagley, 1963 and 1964). The Portuguese family was the colonizing unit, the dominant institution in Brazil that regulated production, politics, administration, social status and defense. Family was regarded not only as the nuclear family (man, wife and children) but also the joint family or an even larger group of relatives, with kinship recognized to the seventh or tenth degree, headed by the patriarch. As Kusnesof and Oppenheimer (1985) maintain, patriarchalism was "the principle that any group, familial or otherwise, will form a hierarchy from the lowest or youngest up to one senior figure under whose protection and dominance it stands, and through whom advancement is obtained" (p. 216).

According to Kuznesof's (1989) study, even less wealthy families shared the traits of the rich patriarchal families. The domination of the father, the protection and isolation of the women, especially the daughters, and the home as a private sphere could be found in these families as well. As early as the 1950s, sociologists were documenting the decline of the agrarian, patriarchal family type and the attendant increase in the importance of the nuclear family (Pierson, 1954). However, regardless of this shift, characteristics of the patriarchal family persist and permeate the lives of Brazilians (Almeida, Carneiro &

Paula, 1987; Azevedo, 1963; Freyre, 1964; Havighurst & Moreira, 1965; Ramos, 1978; Sa, 1947; Wagley, 1963 and 1964; Sarti, 1992).

Gender roles: Division of Labor and Attitudes in Brazil

There are many regional and social class differences regarding family types in Brazil. However, despite the diversity, researchers argue that the patriarchal Brazilian family with traditional gender roles is an ideological model for Brazilians. Even though, as Hahner (1984) indicates, the traditional stereotype of the guarded, pure female was never universally valid and marriage was an unattainable component of social status in the lower classes, the patriarchal ideal still permeates the lives of all. The ideal concepts of femininity and masculinity as well as the relationships between women and men follow the prescribed norms of a patriarchal society. Although Brazil's gender role patterns have been changing, women and men are still regarded as responsible for distinct spheres in life. Home duties and childcare constitute mainly women's responsibilities, while men are responsible for the financial needs of the family. Anthropological studies in poor areas of Brazil demonstrate that despite the type of family constitution, family members adopt a traditional gender role ideology. Scott's (1990) study, done in a poor neighborhood in Recife, the capital of the state of Pernambuco in the northeast part of the country, shows that in poor families where the male presence is not always constant, the expectations continue to involve a strong male dominance, in contrast to the reality of the female's maintenance and support of the family. Similarly, Sarti (1989) indicates that in a poor district of the greater Sao Paulo, the capital of the state of Sao Paulo in the southeast region of the country, different moral codes are used for males and females according to traditional gender roles. A double moral standard is permitted for men, while women have to dedicate themselves to their home, husband and children, or suffer being regarded as immoral. Marriage is essential for determining one's female or male identity in such a way that people who do not marry are regarded as incomplete women or men.

Further, Bonamigo and Rasche (1988) contrasted lower class nuclear families, extended families, and female headed households and found that among those three types of families, women were always responsible for the traditional duties. Socialization of the youngsters also followed that pattern; girls were expected to marry and boys were expected to have a career. Dela-Coleta (1991) cites one of her studies in the state of Minas Gerais, investigating attributions to marital failure with 80 Brazilians of low education. Subjects reported stereotypical sexist reasons for the end of a marriage such as disobedience of the wife towards the husband, the wife not being humble enough or nagging too much or problems of drinking and gambling on the husband's side. Findings showed that women were given greater responsibility for sustaining the marriage.

On the other hand, in the upper classes, there is an attitude that marriage should not deny a woman a career. At the same time there is a common belief, especially among women themselves, that a career should be balanced with the woman's primary responsibility of running the home (Massi, 1991; Miller, 1979). The ambiguity women feel regarding their professional and family lives emerges for the majority of Massi's subjects as a professional crisis. Findings show that most of the subjects, middle class college educated married Brazilian women and also mothers, did not know what to do in their professional lives or acted as if they did not have any degree. Moreover, research with Brazilian university students also indicates some traditionalism. Radice (1987) conducted a study in order to investigate the Brazilian concept of femininity and masculinity, and found that the masculine characteristics are connected to the external world whereas the feminine characteristics, emotional expressive and submissive, are of the internal world. These findings are similar to findings in North America. D'Amorim's (1988) study indicates that undergraduate students still hold stereotypical views regarding family duties. However, different from American subjects, masculine qualities were correlated with feminine professions.

Although attitudes and behaviors continue to be molded by a traditional ideology, changes and achievements towards women's rights have occurred in Brazil, gradually contributing to a transformation in the way society constructs gender. In regard to women's participation in the labor force, there was an increase from the 1970s, when women were a fifth of the hired labor force, to the 1990s, when they have become more than a third of the hired labor force (Bruschini, 1994). Data from the PNADs, Pesquisa Nacional por Amostra de Domicílios (National Research on Household Sample) and from the Instituto Brasileiro de Geografia e Estatística (Brazilian Institute of Geography and Statistics) of 1981 and 1990 indicate that through these years, women's participation in the labor force continued to increase. According to the statistics, before the 1970s there was a higher incidence of female work up to the age of 24, and a decrease beyond that age, as they took charge of family responsibilities. But between 1970 and 1990 women of all ages increased their labor force participation. From 1981 to 1990 women's participation in the commercial, public administration and social sector related to teaching increased. Despite that increase, female workers still have greater difficulty in occupying higher and command posts, and have lower wages compared to men. The salary difference between the sexes increased at higher levels even when there were more women than men in equivalent positions.

In the last four decades education has become more democratic in Brazil and women have greatly benefited (Rosemberg, 1994). In 1970, 42.4% of university students were women. In 1980 the number increased to 49.2% and at the end of the 1980's it went up to 52.9%. There is a relationship between level of education and work outside the house. The probability of women working out of the house is higher when they have a higher level of education. In the public administration area, women show numbers twice as high in terms of high school education and higher education compared to men. In that sector, women occupy positions such as elementary, middle, high school and university teachers. However, men's wages are still higher in spite of women's higher educational levels. Research from the mid-seventies showed that women's participation as professors at the university was much lower than that of men. They represented 23% in the university in contrast to being the great majority, 95%, in elementary levels, 60% in middle school and 5% in high school (Barroso, 1975). The percentages of women in teaching positions reflected the sexual barriers present in Brazilian society. Such patterns seem to be present, however, regarding the small academic availability of courses related to women's issues. In an analysis of the undergraduate and graduate courses taught at one of the main universities of the country, Blay and Conceição (1990) show that women's issues are rarely a topic of study in undergraduate or graduate courses.

Another phenomenon of transformation in Brazilian women's life is the birth rate. In 1984 the birth rate fell to 3.5 children per woman, almost half of what it used to be in 1960 when there were 6.2 children per woman. The new ideal of family seems to be a small one. Two methods of birth control have been widely used, the pill and tubal ligations. The rate of tubal ligations is very high in the whole country. Abortion continues to be legally permitted only in the cases of rape or when there is a threat to the mother's life. In reality, many women have clandestine and illegal abortions, making it difficult to estimate its occurrence. Illegal abortions are widely performed in Brazil, putting many women's lives at risk. It is known that abortion is the fourth cause of maternal mortality.

Regarding Brazilian legislation, until 1962 the constitution placed women at the same level as savages, spendthrifts, and pubescent minors. Their husband's permission was necessary for them to do many things, including exercising a profession or engaging in business. They obtained emancipation through Law 4121 of 1962 under which they attained the condition of companion of their spouse and collaborator in the family responsibilities. They were then authorized to engage in paid professions different from those of their husbands and were free to acquire property. The new constitution of 1988 brought changes to the relationship between men and women stating that both have equal rights and duties in the conjugal relationship

Despite legal accomplishments, citizenship in general, and female citizenship specifically, is still in an embrionary state in Brazil (Saffioti, 1994). Men still have social power over women, and many cases of violence against women go unpunished. Females have become conscious of their rights as women more quickly than men have. Men's slower transformation might be seen in domestic violence: women are victims twice as often as men (Saffioti, 1994). Research suggests there is one case of physical violence against a woman every four minutes and that middle class and upper middle class couples constitute 60% of the cases of violence against women. It is suggested that couples in general are not aware that physical violence constitutes a crime. However, punishment for men who violate women's civil rights is restricted, with only ten per cent of the male aggressors going to trial and, of these, only two per cent convicted.

Role conflict - Sex role in immigration

Gender roles constitute an important factor in every individual's value system. With the move to the new country, values, beliefs, and customs of the immigrant are challenged. Literature on immigration indicates that the disruption of a previous gender roles belief system creates unexpected conflicts in the family structure (Guendelman, 1987; Sluski, 1979).

The changes in women's and men's lives resultant from moving to a new country brings disruption in the conventional relationship between the sexes. Studies of Puerto Ricans (Torres-Matrullo, 1976, 1980), Mexicans (Guendelman, 1987), Cubans (Queralt, 1984), Chicanos (Staples & Mirande, 1980), Dominicans (Pessar, 1984) and Hispanics (Rogler, Cortes & Malgady, 1991) found that due to economic necessity, migration means a first time entry in the labor force for many women. This brings changes to the habitual gender roles in their families.

Through work, women earn some degree of independence and power, which increases their feelings of autonomy and confidence. Such factors mean a break away from the traditional female role, requiring many adjustments in the family. Torres-Matrullo (1976) suggests that the change results in a down grading of the male, whose sense of pride and self-esteem is to a great extent dependent on his culturally prescribed dominant role in the family. Thus, the reversal and reduction of his family role hurts his confidence and self-esteem. Moreover, seeing women as working partners raises the fear that the women's self-interests will override family care. But Guendelman (1987) found that Mexican women perceive their work as strengthening the family rather than focusing on their own self-interests.

Researchers have indicated that the mere fact of the wife's employment outside the home shifts the marital roles towards a more egalitarian pattern (Rogler, Cortes & Magaldy, 1991; Staples & Mirande, 1980). Guendelman (1987) suggests that men increase their participation in activities related to household and childcare in couples who work in the same place, with similar work hours and pooled incomes. The traditional distance between the spouses is diminished resulting in a balance between power relations within the family.

Queralt (1984), however, points out that besides working outside the home, women continue to be responsible for housekeeping and childrearing. The double shift causes considerable stress and role strain on women, resulting in a high rate of divorce within the immigrant population (Queralt, 1984; Parrillo, 1991). Thus, wives' dissatisfaction with the division of labor with their husbands seems to be an important component in marriage dissolution. Landale and Ogena (1993) found that among immigrant couples, women's change in employment status was indicated as one of the reasons for separations, when women started to work in the U.S. and did not work previously to their marriage with their spouse.

In immigrant families where women continue as non-wage earners, the traditional roles are somewhat reinforced. Women become isolated, reclusive and increasingly dependent on their husbands to carry out any activity that demands some knowledge of the language of the host culture (Guendelman, 1987).

The relationships of acculturation and gender role attitudes were investigated at an individual level with Iranians and Puerto Ricans living in the U.S. In the case of Iranian female immigrants, Hannassab (1991) indicates that the more acculturated the individuals, the more liberal they are toward sex roles. Similar findings were indicated by Torres-Matrullo (1980) in a study with Puerto Rican men. The subjects' changes in sex-role conceptions were shown to be influenced by their levels of acculturation.

However, in another study the situation seems a little more complex. Ghaffarian (1987) suggests that although Iranian men are more acculturated than Iranian women toward the American society, they still hold traditional views of women's roles. The women, in contrast, although less acculturated and presenting traditional behavior, show modern values concerning the female role. The author suggests that the women have new ideas about women's roles but are not ready to behave accordingly. Similar to Iranians, a dualistic practice is also adopted by South Asian women. They apply traditionalism to home and childcare, whereas they have contemporary attitudes toward education, career, and goals for themselves and their daughters (Naidoo and Davis, 1988). Such studies support what other researchers have suggested, that there may be a different degree of acculturation in public versus private behaviors (Clark, Kaufman & Pierce, 1976). Melville's (1978) study with Mexican immigrant women suggested that some women who had become more liberal in their gender role attitudes became unsatisfied with their relationships to their husbands, who had not changed in the same way.

Hondagneu-Sotelo (1994), in a study of 26 Mexican immigrant families, states that families become less patriarchal as a consequence of the immigration experience itself. She contends that couples became more egalitarian both through their immigration and settlement experiences, as well as by women's increase and men's decrease in economic contributions to the family. Thus, new patterns of behavior are linked to the arrangements of family migration and the fact that migration is a gendered process. Women experience new role responsibilities when their husbands leave, which promotes their change towards greater autonomy and independence, together with the formation of a women's network. Similarly, men who live for many years in "bachelor communities" take responsibility for some of the housework when they rejoin the family. The author states that these changes "are not related to any 'modernizing' Anglo influence or acculturation process. Most Mexican immigrants live their lives in the United States encapsulated in relatively segregated jobs and well-defined immigrant communities" (p.195).

Family pressure to maintain the status quo of women's roles is clearly depicted towards girls in the case of Italian immigrants in Canada (Danziger, 1974). The study indicates that parents employ a conservative attitude regarding the socialization of the girls to sustain the traditional norms of family life. The parents allow little autonomy to the girls, and maintain high expectations about involvement in household activities. Similarly, a differentiation between the socialization of boys and girls was found among Armenians in Australia (Kirkland, 1984).

Woon (1986) in a study of Sino-Vietnamese families in Canada, shows that family pressure regarding gender roles is related to socioeconomic mobility in the new land. Families that suffered downward mobility still maintained a traditional arrangement of roles. In contrast, in the families that moved their social economic status upwardly, husbands treated their wives as equal partners.

This chapter described the concept of gender roles, attitudes and division of labor in booth the North American and Brazilian cultures. In addition, gender role changes with immigration and the relation between gender role and marital satisfaction were addressed.

CHAPTER 4
Method

Participants

The sample for this research consisted of 50 Brazilian immigrant married couples (50 females and 50 males) who participated in the research from the period of December 1996 to July 1997. The families were from various Brazilian communities in the greater Boston area. To participate in the study, families had to have arrived at least six months to fifteen years earlier in the US, at least one child ranging from less than one year old to adolescent age, a male and a female spouse living together and been engaged in Brazil. The subjects were recruited through community leaders linked to associations serving Portuguese speakers, a Brazilian Catholic priest, a Brazilian minister, acquaintances, a Brazilian radio show and through the 'snow ball' process. Such a procedure is the suggested one when dealing with a population for which there is both a lack of statistical data and many undocumented residents (Cornelius, 1982). One hundred and sixty six families were listed, and the researcher contacted one hundred and forty nine by telephone. For various reasons (disconnected or wrong phone numbers, lack of time or interest, husband not interested, not meeting the criteria for the research sample, having already reached the needed number of families) some families were not included. The researcher briefly explained on the phone the purpose of the study as described on the letter of consent, which was presented to the participants before the interview (Appendix A).

The average age of the wives in the sample at the time of the interview was 35.38 (SD = 6.30) with a range of 23 to 53, and the average age of the husbands was 38.28 (SD = 6.13) with a range of 28 to 57. Twenty percent of the couples had been married in Brazil and left immediately thereafter to the United States; 8% lived together in Brazil from one month to four months and the other 72% had lived together in Brazil from seven months to twenty two years before moving to the United States. On average, the couples had lived together 11.94 years (SD = 6.11) and had lived an average of 7.5 years in the U.S, with a minimum of one year to a maximum of 13 years. Fourteen percent (N=7) of the men were in their second marriage; two percent (N=1) were in their third conjugal relationship, while the majority, 84% (N=42), were in their first marriage. For the women, only 6% (N=3) were in their second marriage, while the majority, 94% (N=47), were in their first marriage. All had at least one child and a maximum of three children living with them.

In terms of the sample education, of the women studied, 10% had an education below the seventh grade level, 4% had completed junior high, 8% had completed some high school, 36% were high school graduates, 22% had partial college or specialized training and 20% had college degrees. Ten percent of the men had completed less than seventh grade; 8% graduated from junior high, 10% had partial high school; 30% had graduated from high school; 30% had partial college or specialized training and 12%

Method

had graduated from college. Such percentages represent a sharp contrast to the Brazilian population's educational status similar to what Margolis (1994) found. More than 50% of the couples lived in the state of Minas Gerais in Brazil before immigrating to the U.S.. Others came from Espirito Santo, Goiás, Paraná, Rio de Janeiro, Rio Grande do Sul and São Paulo. They came mainly from middle size towns (100,000 to 500,000 people). In terms of religious affiliation, most of the sample was either Catholic (54%), or Protestant (35%). Five percent were Spiritist and 6% were not religious.

In most of the families in the study both the husband and wife worked. According to Hollingshead's (1975) categories, 16% of the wives were unskilled workers, 64% semiskilled workers, 14% skilled manual workers or managers and minor professionals, and 6% housewives or unemployed. Among the semiskilled workers 30 women worked as housecleaners for American families. Ten percent of men did menial service or were farm laborers; 26% were unskilled workers; 44% were semiskilled workers; 14% were skilled manual workers and smaller business owners; 4% were technicians and semiprofessionals and 25% were managers or minor professionals. Among the semiskilled workers 10 men worked as housecleaners together with their wives. Women were mainly from a semiskilled worker and machine operator social class, (42%, n= 21) which corresponds to the fourth category in Hollingshead's five category social status index (1 being highest and 5 being lowest). Twenty-eight per cent (n=14) were from the third category of skilled craftsmen, clerical and sales workers class; 18% were from the lowest (5) class of unskilled laborers, menial service workers; and 12% were from the second highest class (2) of medium business, minor professional and technical professional. Similarly, 44% of the men were from semiskilled worker and machine operator category (4), 30% were from the skilled craftsmen, clinical and sales workers class (3), 22% were from the lowest, unskilled laborers, menial services category (5) and only 4% were from the second highest medium business, minor professional and technical class (2). Their salaries per week ranged from none (in the case of three women who did not work outside the house) to $800 for the women with an average of $400 and from $213 to $1,200 for the men with an average of $542. Women worked an average of 36 hours per week and men an average of 51 hours per week. In Brazil 30% of the women either did not work out of the house or were unemployed as opposed to 6% in the U.S. and 24% of the men were unemployed in Brazil whereas none were in the U.S.

Study Design and Procedures

For the present, a study questionnaire designed with a total of 123 questions, including open-ended questions and five self-report acculturation and gender role measures, was used. Therefore, both qualitative and quantitative data was obtained. The researcher went to all the families' houses, with the exception of one female participant who was interviewed at her work place. Spouses were interviewed separately, since the objective was to have their individual perception of the household. An average of four to five hours was spent in each house.

Prior to each interview the participants were given a consent form to sign (see Appendix Z), in which the researcher explained the purpose of the study, attested to confidentiality and informed them that they could interrupt the interview at any time or not answer any question. Along with the consent form each participant completed a separate sheet with his or her name and address. The purpose of collecting this data was to provide participants a brief summary of the research findings. By reading and explaining each measure used, the researcher guaranteed that each participant understood the questionnaire, especially the fixed-response questions. In that way, problems in the administration of questionnaires with fixed-response format and scales with a population that is not used to such procedures, as has been shown by other researchers (Pick-de-Weiss and David, 1981), were avoided. The questionnaire was administered in Portuguese since most participants were not fluent in English.

Each family received a voucher worth $20 to be used in ethnic stores and restaurants. All interviews were taped and later transcribed. Side comments made by the participants when answering the scales were included. After each visit, the researcher wrote notes on the organization of the house and personal impressions of the family regarding their response to the interview situation.

Measures

In the research, measures of gender roles and acculturation were used as independent constructs and marital satisfaction as the dependent construct. All measures were written in English and translated to Portuguese by four bilingual speakers. The translations were compared to reach a common ground and clarity. The questionnaire was piloted with three Brazilian immigrants (two women and one man in their mid thirties) and discussed with two Brazilian community leaders.

After that, it was adapted to a more colloquial and less academic language than used on the original scales. The final format was then established.

The following two measures regarding gender roles were applied:

The Attitude Towards Women Scale (AWS): Developed by Spence and Helmreich (1972), the AWS is the most commonly used measure of attitudes toward women in psychological studies. Among the three versions of the AWS in existence, the present study used the 15-item version to which Spence and Helmreich (1972) reported a correlation .91 in relation to the longer 55-item version. A coefficient alpha of .89 for the shorter version was also reported. The instrument was once applied to a Brazilian college student sample but the researcher, when asked about its translation was unable to find it (Levine, R. V. & West, L., 1979). In general, items pertain to the rights, roles and privileges of women and assess sex-role ideology. As Spence and Hahn (1997) explain, the AWS intends to capture people's beliefs about responsibilities, privileges, and behaviors in different spheres that traditionally are divided along gender lines but can be shared equally by men and women. The scale does not address beliefs about men's and women's cognitive abilities, personality characteristics or attitudes toward political issues relevant to gender such as abortion, the feminist movement or anti-discriminatory legislation. The scale assesses beliefs about responsibilities and rights for women versus those for men. It ranges from liberal or non-traditional to traditional attitudes towards women. On all three versions, items are accompanied by four responses running from "agree strongly" (3) to "disagree strongly" (0). Four new questions were added, three involving sexual desire and one regarding preference for a male boss. Total scores on the adapted AWS scale range from 0 to 57, with 0 indicating traditional attitudes towards women and 57 liberal attitudes towards women.

The Household Task and ChildCare measure (Baruch and Barnett, 1986; Brody,1993). This measure consists of a checklist of 10 household tasks, six of them being stereotypically female (cleaning the house, meal preparation, meal clean-up, grocery shopping, laundry and social life organization) and four being stereotypically male (yard work, home repairs, car maintenance and repairs, bill paying). Childcare is measured through 15 tasks such as staying home with a sick child, going to school events and so on. Some new questions were added for the stereotypically female tasks (folds and puts away clean clothes, makes the bed) and to the stereotypically male tasks (takes out the garbage). Thus the adapted scale comprised a total of 30 questions of which 15 regarded childcare, 9 feminine household tasks, 5 masculine household tasks and one question rating the satisfaction with spouse's division of labor. The original percentage rating scale was adapted to a pie chart divided in ten parts. Participants were asked to make four ratings on the pie chart form by coloring the parts corresponding to the amount of time he/she spent in each task, the amount of time his/her spouse spent performing the task, the amount of time he/she performed the task together with his/her spouse, and the amount of time a third person spent performing the task (a person that lived or at least was three times a week with the family and shared household or childcare tasks). Based on the types of tasks, six scores were created: ratio scores of the traditionally female chores done by wives and husbands, ratio scores of the traditionally male chores done by wives and husbands, and ratio scores of the childcare tasks. The respondent rated satisfaction with spouse's division of labor on a 1 (extremely satisfied) to 7 (extremely unsatisfied) scale. Reliability of this measure has been demonstrated in that husbands and wives' scores are significantly correlated (Brody, 1993). Predicted validity has been demonstrated by findings that scores on the measures relate to children's gender roles (Baruch and Barnett, 1986).

Three measures were used to assess acculturation:

Short Acculturation Scale for Hispanics. An adaptation of the 12-item acculturation scale for Hispanics (Marin, Sabogal, et. al., 1987) was used. Three factors are assessed: language use, media, and ethnic social relations. One question of the original questionnaire (language used as a child) was omitted since the sample constituted only first generation immigrants who therefore spoke their native language as a child. Two other questions were modified: one question that included languages read and spoken was modified to include only languages spoken; the other modified question regarded languages spoken at home. That question was divided in two other questions, one regarding the language spoken with children at home and the other language spoken with spouse at home. Studies have shown that immigrant's children easily learn the second language (Woon, 1986; Wong, 1985). Moreover, I had observed in a previous study with Brazilian immigrant families that children spoke English and Portuguese at home (DeBiaggi, 1992). Further, four new questions were added to assess other factors suggested by Mendoza (1989): cultural familiarity and activities (food preference), cultural identification and pride (ethnic identity, choice of neighbors' nationality) and extra family language (language spoken with coworkers). The seventeen items are accompanied by five responses ranging from 1, "only Portuguese" or "all Brazilians", depending whether it assessed language or other factors, to 5, "only English" or "all Americans". The validity and reliability coefficients (alpha coefficient .92) for the short acculturation scale for Hispanics are comparable to those obtained for other published scales. Separate validations for Mexican Americans and Central Americans showed similar results (Marin, Sabogal, et. al., 1987). Acculturation was measured through the total sum of scores of all items ranging from 17 to 85, with 17 indicating low acculturation and 85 indicating high acculturation.

Length of time in US. Subjects were asked when they arrived in the US.

English Language Proficiency. English language proficiency was measured using an adaptation of the six-point scale developed by Sales (1984) which measures both speaking and listening comprehension from 0, no knowledge of English at all, to 6, totally fluent, like a native American. The scale was based on categories developed by language examiners at the US Foreign Service Institute. Sales reported a coefficient alpha of .95 for the scale. After the pilot study the final format considered speaking and listening as one since pilot subjects reported being confused by the original structure in which they were asked to rate themselves in both aspects.

One measure of marital satisfaction was used:
Dyadic Adjustment Scale. This is a 32-item scale developed by Spanier (1976) and designed to measure the quality of adjustment in marriage and similar dyadic relationships. It is the most frequently used and well-researched instrument for assessing relationship satisfaction. It gives total adjustment score and four subscales: dyadic consensus, dyadic satisfaction, dyadic cohesion and affectional expression. Reliability studies indicate good internal consistency among items, and stable scores for the total measure and two of the subscales. Dyadic satisfaction is measured by items pertaining to the respondents extent of agreement on ten items such as confiding in one's partner and regretting being married, on a scale ranging from 0 (never) to 5 (all of the time). Dyadic cohesion is measured on items addressing shared activities such as laughing together or having a stimulating exchange of ideas, in which respondents indicate the extent of agreement on a scale ranging from 0 (never) to 5 (more often) on four items, and ranging from 0 (none of them) to 5 (all of them) on one item. Dyadic consensus is measured by items in 15 areas, such as handling family finances, friends and career decisions in which respondents indicate the extent of agreement on a scale ranging from 0 (always disagree) to 5 (always agree). Affective expression is measured on items that measure the respondents extent of agreement on showing love and sexual desire, on a response format with two points 0(yes) and 1(no). However, lower reliability has been reported for the affectional expression and dyadic cohesion subscales (Kramer and Conoley, 1992). For the purpose of this research only the overall scores were utilized. Total scores may range from 0 to 151, with 0 indicating stressed marriages and 151 indicating optimum marital adjustment.

Demographic and immigration open ended and fixed-response questions:

Twenty three questions were developed in order to obtain demographics (date of birth, education, number of children and so on), marriage and cohabitation data (how long married or together), aspects of the migration history (when arrived in the U.S.), migration satisfaction and family immigration (wishes to go back to Brazil at present, would recommend coming to U.S. to other immigrant families, would do it all over again). SES was addressed by asking subjects their educational level and present occupation.

The following specific hypotheses were tested:

1. The more acculturated women and men are, the less they will show traditional attitudes towards males' and females' gender roles.
2. The more acculturated women are, the more they will be dissatisfied with their husband's percentage of housework.
3. Husbands that share more housework and childcare will be more acculturated and will have more liberal attitudes toward women's role.
4. Marital adjustment will be higher for wives and husbands when both have similar gender role attitudes than when they have dissimilar gender role attitudes.
5. Level of acculturation and gender role will interact in predicting marital satisfaction: higher levels of acculturation and more liberal gender roles will predict high marital satisfaction, and lower levels of acculturation and traditional gender roles will predict high marital satisfaction.

6. Wives will be more liberal in their gender roles in a shorter period of time than will husbands.
7. Men's gender role attitudes will positively correlate with their wives' gender role attitudes. However, men's behaviors will not significantly correlate with their wives' attitudes.
8. Men's attitudes and behaviors will not significantly correlate.

Chapter 5
Results

The first section of this chapter presents the descriptive results of the variables studied (acculturation, gender roles and marital satisfaction) and comparisons between wives and husbands. Then the relationships between measures of acculturation and measures of gender roles are explored. The third section investigates the research hypotheses looking at the relationship between wives' and husbands' acculturation, gender roles and marital satisfaction. The following section examines groups of couples formed according to their acculturation and the relation of the groups to gender roles and marital satisfaction. The final section looks at qualitative results gathered from the interviews.

Descriptive Statistics

Table 1 provides ranges, means, standard deviations and medians of the wives and husbands' variables used to investigate acculturation (scores on acculturation scale, English proficiency, time in the U.S.), gender role attitudes and behavior (feminine household tasks, masculine household tasks, childcare tasks) and marital satisfaction.

Table 1 Range, Mean, Standard Deviation, and Median of Husbands and Wives' Scores

Variable	N	Range	M	SD	Mdn
Wives' Acculturation	50	25-61	42.06	7.83	42
Husbands' Acculturation	50	24-60	42.90	8.70	43.5
Wives' English Proficiency	50	0-4	2,30	1,07	2
Husbands' English Proficiency	50	0-5	2,54	1,18	2,5
Wives' Time in the U.S.	50	1-13	6,45	3,13	6.91
Husbands' Time in the U.S.	50	1-13	7,65	2,99	8
Wives' Gender Role Attitudes	50	26-50	39.30	6.51	39
Husbands' Gender Role Attitudes	50	21-48	35.08	6.21	35
Wives' Feminine Household Tasks	50	.31-.97	.75	.13	.75
Husbands' Feminine household Tasks	50	.03-.60	.33	.14	.33
Wives' Masculine household Tasks	50	.31-1.00	.29	.16	.27
Husbands' Masculine Household Tasks	50	.31-.75	.76	.18	.77
Wives' Childcare tasks	50	.55-1.00	.77	.10	.77
Husbands' Childcare tasks	50	.15-.89	.47	.18	.46
Wives' Marital Satisfaction	50	51-136	104.92	17.87	106
Husbands' Marital Satisfaction	50	78-135	108.88	13.72	107.5

Results

The acculturation level was obtained through the total sum of scores of the short acculturation measure. Scores ranged from 17 to 85. Seventeen indicated the lowest level of acculturation and 85 indicated the highest. Subjects were asked about contact, socialization and preferred ethnicity of people with whom respondents interact; language spoken and language preference in different settings and with different people (co-workers, own children and spouse); language and preference in media use (TV, radio, video); food preference and self ethnic identification. The answering scale ranged from "only Brazilian" or "only Portuguese" to "only American" or "only English." On measures of preferred contact and socialization (Americans or Brazilians), using English or Portuguese media, eating American or Brazilian foods, and identifying oneself as either American or Brazilian, the middle option, "half and half" or "both equally" was most often preferred. The sample means of males (M=42.06) and females (M= 42.9) suggest a mid-point acculturation level in the behaviors measured, indicating a tendency in the sample to consider as important both Brazilian and American cultural aspects of life. In order to test for gender differences in acculturation a Paired-sample t-test was conducted. However, no significant difference was found (t=.78, p=.43), indicating that wives and husbands are similar in acculturation level.

Regarding English proficiency, which was measured through a scale ranging from 0 "no knowledge or understanding of English at all" to 5 "totally fluent, like a native American" the sample population means both for wives (M= 2.30) and husbands (M= 2.54) showed that the average immigrant tends to rate himself or herself at a level indicating he or she is fluent enough to handle limited work requirements and most social situations (corresponds to level 2 on the proficiency scale). Paired-sample t-tests showed that couples are not significantly different on their English proficiency (t=1.17, p=.25).

Time in the U.S. was obtained by subtracting date of arrival in U.S. from date of the interview. A paired sample t-test indicates that husbands and wives' time in U.S. significantly differ (t=3.97, p=.000) in the direction that husbands have been longer in the U.S. (M=7,65) than wives (M=6,45).

The adapted version of the Attitudes Toward Women scale (Spence & Helmreich, 1972) used to measure gender role attitudes, included the 15-item version of the original Attitudes Toward Women scale and four added questions for the present study. The total scores on the adapted scale range from 0 to 57 whereas in the original 15-item version, scores range from 0 to 45. In both versions 0 corresponds to traditional/conservative attitudes and the highest score to more liberal/feminist attitudes toward women. To test for differences between the sexes a paired sample t-test was conducted showing that wives and husbands significantly differ on gender role attitudes (t= -4.05, p=.000). The means of the present sample (M= 39.3 for wives and M=35.08 for husbands) show a tendency for wives to be more liberal than their husbands. Many studies have found that women consistently score as more liberal than men on their gender role attitudes (Spence & Hahn, 1997; Twenge, 1997).

Wives and husbands significantly differed on their household and childcare tasks, which were measured through an adapted version of the Household Task and ChildCare (Baruch and Barnett, 1986; Brody,1993). Household tasks were composed of stereotypically feminine chores such as washing the dishes, preparing the meals and taking care of houseplants and stereotypically masculine chores such as maintaining the car and taking out the garbage. Further, childcare tasks included taking children to birthday parties, buying children's clothes and discipline. Paired sample t-tests indicated that husbands and wives significantly differed in performance of feminine household tasks (t=-13,67, p=.000), masculine household tasks (t=10,44, p=.000) and childcare (t=-8,91, p=.000). Means of the constructs indicate that wives perform more feminine chores around the house (M=.75) than do husbands (M=.33) and do more childcare (M=.77) than husbands (M=.47). Husbands were more involved in performance of typically masculine tasks (M=.76) than their wives (M=.29).

Marital satisfaction was measured through total scores on the Dyadic Adjustment scale (Spanier, 1976) which ranges from 0, or stressed marriages, to 151, indicating an optimum marital relationship. The scale addresses dyadic consensus (e.g.: extent of agreement or disagreement on "Career decisions", "household tasks," "making major decisions" and so on), dyadic satisfaction (amount of time spouses confide in each other, think of or discuss divorce, get on each other's nerves, and so on), affectional expression (sex relations, demonstrations of affection), and dyadic cohesion (amount of time spouses laugh together, have a stimulating exchange of ideas and so on). Other studies using American clinical and community populations (Morell, 1997) describe the average distressed spouse scoring under 90 points (M=89.40) and the average nondistressed spouse scoring over 100 points (M= 115.65). Spanier (1976) contrasted a divorced sample to a married sample and significant differences were found between their means (M= 70.7 and M= 114.8 respectively). Wives' and husbands' average score (M=104.92 and M=108.88 respectively) in the present study appear to be near the nondistressed average score. In order to test for gender differences a paired sample t-test was performed. No significant difference was found; wives and husbands had similar marital satisfaction (t=1.58, p=.12).

In order explore the relations between acculturation measures (Short acculturation scale, time in the U.S. and English proficiency) and between gender roles measures (Attitudes toward women and household and childcare tasks) Pearson correlations were performed.

Correlation between measures of Acculturation
For females (n=50), the results indicate that the more acculturated women, the more English they know (r=.49, p=.003). How long they have been in the new country is not associated to their acculturation (r=-.12, p=.42). But women's English proficiency does improve with time in the United States, (r=.41, p=.003).

For the male sample (n=50), the results also indicate that acculturation is related to English proficiency, (r=.55, p<.001) and English proficiency improves with time in the U.S. (r=.32, p=.02). There is no relation between time in the U.S. and acculturation, (r=-.11, p=.45). When taking off two outlier observations, the results become the following: English Proficiency is correlated to acculturation (r = .62, p = .0001), but time in the U.S. is correlated neither to English proficiency (r=.21, p=.15) or acculturation, (r= .21, p = .15).

Correlation between measures of gender roles
For the women there tended to be a relation between gender role attitudes and performance of feminine tasks (r=.24, p=.10). Thus, as women perform more feminine tasks they tend to become more liberal. No relation was found between their gender role attitude and childcare tasks

(r=.10, p=.50). Women's gender role attitudes were also not associated with performing masculine household tasks (r=.17, p=.23). An association was found between their feminine tasks and childcare tasks (r=.45, p=.001). As involvement with household tasks increased women did more childcare. Further, an association was found between feminine tasks and masculine tasks (r= .37, p= .0007). As women performed more feminine tasks they also performed more masculine tasks at home. Brody and Flanagan (in press) found similar relationships.

For men no relation was found between their gender role attitudes and performance of feminine tasks (r= .15, p= .43). Thus, for men being more liberal did not mean that they performed more feminine tasks. Moreover no relation was found between their gender role attitudes and childcare tasks (r=.17, p=.25). Similarly, their gender role attitudes were not associated to masculine tasks (r=-.51, p=.73). Thus, whether men were more liberal or traditional was not related to their performance of feminine or masculine household tasks nor childcare at home. However, a relationship was found between their performance of feminine tasks and childcare tasks (r=.5, p=.0002). When men were more involved in feminine household tasks they were more involved with childcare as well. The performance of masculine tasks and feminine tasks were not associated (r=.14, p=.35).

<u>Hypothesis #1 The more acculturated women and men are, the less they will show traditional attitudes towards males and females.</u>
Through Pearson correlations it was found that for wives there was no relation between their acculturation and attitudes towards women (r=.15; p=.28). Becoming more acculturated was not associated to becoming more liberal

for wives. But for husbands their acculturation was related to their gender role attitudes (r=.31; p=.03). As the husbands acculturated they became more liberal. Further, husbands' and wives' gender role attitudes were correlated, (r= .33 ; p= .02). These findings support the first hypothesis of the study for the husbands, who became more liberal as they acculturated, but not for the wives', for whom no relation between their acculturation and liberalism was found.

Hypothesis #2. The more acculturated wives are, the more they will be dissatisfied with their husband's percentage of housework.
No relation was found between wives' satisfaction with division of household tasks and their acculturation (r=-.04, p=.78). Wives' being more or less acculturated was not associated with dissatisfaction with their husband's percentage of household labor. These findings do not support the second hypothesis.

Hypothesis #3. Husbands that share more childcare and housework will be more acculturated and will have more liberal attitudes toward women's roles.
Husband's acculturation was associated with an increase in performance of childcare tasks (r= .39, p= .0045). As husbands acculturated they were more involved in taking care of their children. But no relation was found between acculturation and feminine household tasks (r= -.03, p= .84). Further, no relation was found between acculturation and masculine tasks, (r=-.08, p=.57). Being more or less acculturated was not connected to performing more or less masculine household labor. Therefore, the third hypothesis is partially supported; as husbands acculturated they did share more childcare with

their wives but their acculturation had no influence on their performance of neither feminine nor masculine household tasks at home.

Hypothesis #4. Marital adjustment will be higher for wife and husband when both have similar gender role attitudes than when they have dissimilar gender role attitudes.
Difference scores between wives and husbands' attitudes towards women were obtained and then correlated to wives and husbands' marital adjustment. No relation was found either with the signed difference score (r=.103, p=.48), nor the absolute value difference score (r=.187, p=.193). Having similar gender role attitudes, such as both being traditional or liberal, or dissimilar gender role attitudes, such as one spouse being liberal and the other traditional, had no influence on couple's marital satisfaction. The findings did not support the fourth hypothesis.

Hypothesis #5. Level of acculturation, sex of participant and gender role will predict marital satisfaction.
Multiple regression analyses were conducted separately for husbands and wives to test the relative contributions of acculturation and gender role to predicted marital satisfaction. Husbands and wives' marital satisfaction were used as outcome measures. Three items, women's and men's gender role attitudes, their acculturation, and interaction terms between acculturation and gender role attitudes were used as predictors. Table 2 indicates that these six constructs together account for 25% of the variance in wives marital satisfaction scores, [$F(6,43)=2.42$, $p=.04$]. Husband's acculturation (t =3.34 , $p=.002$), husband's gender role attitudes (t=3.17, $p=.003$) and husband's interaction term between

acculturation and gender role attitudes (t=-3.20, p=.003) are significant and the interaction term between women's acculturation and gender role attitudes (t=1.85, p=.07) tended towards significance. Thus, wives' satisfaction with their marital relationship may be predicted through the level of acculturation and gender role attitudes of both spouses in general, and the husbands' in particular.

Table 2
Summary of First Regression Analysis of Variables Predicting Wives Marital Satisfaction (N=50)

Variable	B	SE B	t
Wives' Gender role attitudes	-3.76	2.32	-1.62
Wives' Acculturation	-4.32	2.25	-1.91*
Wives' Gender role attitudes vs. Acculturation	.10	.05	1.85*
Husbands' Gender role attitudes	7.77	2.45	3.17**
Husbands' Acculturation	6.46	1.93	3.34**
Husbands' Gender role attitudes vs. acculturation	-.18	.06	-3.20**

Note R^2 = .25
a. Predictors: (constant), Wives' ATW, Wives' Acculturation, Wives' Interaction Term, Husband's ATW, Husband's Acculturation, Husband's Interaction Term
b. Dependent variable: Wives' Marital Satisfaction
* $p<.08$
** $p<.003$

Results 83

A model without wives' interaction term was tested but it was not significant at the .05 level (p=.08) and all independent variables were weaker, making the first model a better predictor. In order to understand the interaction between acculturation and gender role attitudes of husbands to wives' marital satisfaction, regression analysis were performed. Two groups of husbands with higher and lower acculturation were obtained through median splits of the whole male sample. Wives' marital satisfaction was regressed on each group. Tables 3 and 4 indicate that wives marital satisfaction regressed on husbands' gender role attitudes, both for the more acculturated husbands and for the less acculturated husbands, were non-significant. The regressions indicate that for the less acculturated husbands, as they became more liberal on their gender role attitudes, wives were more satisfied in their marital relationship, whereas for the more acculturated husbands, as they became more liberal, wives were somewhat less satisfied.

Table 3
Summary Regression Analysis of Gender Role Attitude of More Acculturated Husbands PredictingWives' Marital Satisfaction (N=50)

Variable	B	SE B	t
Husbands' gender role attitudes	-.42	.61	.47

Note R^2 = .02
a. Predictors: (constant), Husband's gender role attitudes
b. Dependent variable: Wives' Marital Satisfaction

Table 4
Summary Regression Analysis of Gender Role Attitude of Less Acculturated Husbands Predicting Wives Marital Satisfaction (N=50)

Variable	B	SEB	t
Husbands' gender role attitudes	.91	.59	2.39

Note R^2 = .09

    a. Predictors: (constant), Husband's gender role attitudes
    b. Dependent variable: Wives' Marital Satisfaction

The same constructs (gender role attitudes, acculturation and interaction terms of acculturation and gender role attitudes of husbands and wives) were used in a multiple regression analysis to test husbands' marital satisfaction. The model was non-significant (F=.36, p=.90) and none of the constructs were significant or approached significance.

To test whether childcare tasks, feminine household tasks or masculine household tasks performed by husbands and wives predicted wives and husbands' marital satisfaction, multiple regression analyses were conducted. Husbands' marital satisfaction was regressed on the six constructs mentioned above. The model was non-significant (p= .37). However, Table 5 provides evidence that feminine household tasks performed by husbands approached significance (t= 1.91, p =.06) which indicates that it contributes to men's marital satisfaction, whereas no other construct was significant. Further, previous analyses showed a positive Pearson correlation between men's marital satisfaction and feminine household tasks (r=.34, p=.02).

Results

Table 5
Summary of Second Regression Analysis of Variables Predicting Husband's Marital Satisfaction (N=50)

Variable	B	Std.Error	T
Wives' Childcare	13.91	23.82	.56
Husbands' Childcare	-.07	14.58	.10
Wives' Feminine Tasks	-7.60	21.49	-.35
Husbands' Feminine Tasks	36.11	18.89	1.91*
Wives' Masculine Tasks	2.95	21.76	.14
Husbands' Masculine Tasks	-7.96	22.92	-.35

a. Predictors: (constant), Wives' Childcare, Husband's Childcare, Wives' Feminine tasks, Husband's Feminine Tasks, Wives Masculine Tasks, Husband's Masc. Tasks
b. Dependent variable: Husband's Marital Satisfaction
* p<.08

Wives' marital satisfaction was regressed on the six constructs. The six variables contributed to 27% of the variance in marital satisfaction. Although the multiple regression is significant [F=2.70. p=.003], as indicated on Table 6, only the construct of childcare tasks performed by husbands approached significance (p=.10) indicating that wives are more satisfied in their marriages when their husbands take care of their children.

Further, Pearson correlations were performed between wives' marital satisfaction and husbands' childcare tasks and a relation was found (r=.41, p=.003). Wives' marital satisfaction increased when husbands spent more time taking care of their children. A relation between wives marital satisfaction and husband's performance of household tasks was also found (r=.35, p=.013). Wives' are more satisfied with their marital relationship when husbands perform feminine household tasks.

Table 6
Summary of Third Regression Analysis of Variables Predicting Wives' Marital Satisfaction (N=50)

Variable	B	SE B	t
Wives' Childcare	16.18	28.28	.57
Husband's Childcare	29.50	17.31	1.70*
Wives' Feminine Tasks	9.70	25.52	.38
Husband's Feminine Tasks	35.90	22.43	1.60**
Wives' Masculine Tasks	32.70	25.84	1.27
Husband's Masculine Tasks	25.52	27.21	.94

Note R^2 = .27
a. Predictors: (constant), Wives' Childcare, Husband's Childcare, Wives' Feminine tasks, Husband's Feminine Tasks, Wives Masculine Tasks, Husband's Masculine Tasks
b. Dependent variable: Husband's Marital Satisfaction
* p=.10
** p=.12

Hypothesis #6. Wives will be more liberal in their gender roles a shorter period of time since their arrival than will husbands.

To test whether women and men differed in their attitudes toward women, a t-test was conducted. A significant difference was found between women and men's gender role attitudes (t=3.32, p=.001) with women having higher gender role attitudes ($\underline{M}$=39.30) than men ($\underline{M}$=35.08). Women had a more liberal attitude towards women than men did. Further, Pearson correlations were performed between wives' attitudes towards women and time in the U.S. but no relation was found (r= .16, p= .28).

In addition, to test whether there was a difference in attitudes towards women between women who had been a shorter period of time (< 6.83 years) and men who had been a longer period of time in the U.S. (> 8 years), a t-test was conducted between those two groups. The groups were obtained through median splits of time in the U.S. A significant difference was found (t=2.10, p=.04) and women who had been a shorter time in the U.S. had higher ATW ($\underline{M}$=39.12) scores than men who had been in the U.S. for a longer time ($\underline{M}$=35.40). Women have a more liberal gender role attitude than men regardless of how long they have been in the U.S.

Thus, time in the new country is related to an increase in liberalism only for men and not for women. Independent of time, women are more liberal than men. Even when men become more liberal they are not still as liberal as women.

<u>Hypothesis #7. Men's attitudes will positively correlate with their wives' attitudes but men's behaviors will not significantly correlate with their wives' attitudes.</u>

Pearson correlations were performed between men's and wives' attitudes towards women and a positive relation was found (r= .32, p= .02). No relation was found between wives gender role attitudes and men's performance of feminine tasks (r=.21, p=.15) nor their performance of masculine tasks (r=-.03, p=.83). However, there is an association between women's gender role attitudes and men's performance of childcare tasks (r=.34, p=.02). Hypothesis seven was partially supported by these findings since women's liberal gender role attitudes did not relate to men's performance of feminine and masculine household tasks but did relate to men's care of their children.

Hypothesis #8. Men's gender role attitudes and behaviors will not significantly correlate.
A Pearson correlation analysis between men's attitudes towards women and performance of feminine household tasks was conducted and no relation was found (r=.11, p=.43) Men's gender role attitudes and the amount of childcare they did were also not associated (r=.17, p=.25). These findings support the expectation that men's gender role attitudes and behaviors such as doing feminine household tasks and childcare tasks, were not associated.

Post-hoc Analysis
A cluster analysis of the fifty couples using Ward's minimum variance criterion was conducted in order to determine similar groups of couples from the whole sample. The analysis was based on wives and husband's acculturation factors such as acculturation scale score, time in the U.S., satisfaction with immigration and English proficiency. The Ward's criterion at each step of the clustering process merges groups so that the selected group has the smallest variance. The elements of each group are closest in minimum variance. The dendogram (Figure 1) shows the four groups that were formed.

Results

Figure 1
Cluster Analysis Grouping of Couples Based on Acculturation Factors

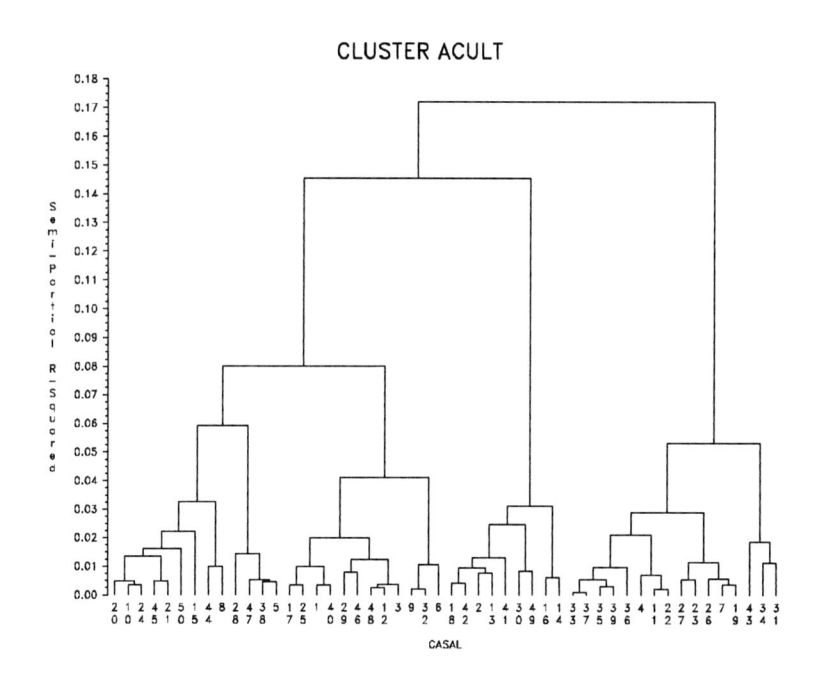

CLUSTER ACULT

Table 7 shows the means of the groups on the factors by which the groups were formed (acculturation scale score, time in the U.S., satisfaction with immigration and English proficiency).

Table 7
Four Cluster Groups and Means of Acculturation Factors

	Group 1	Group 2	Group 3	Group 4
N	13	12	9	16
Wives' Acculturation scale score	36.7	37.3	46.1	47.7
Husband's Acculturation scale score	39.5	35.1	47.2	49.1
Wives' time in U.S	6.55	7.23	2.08	8.22
Husbands time in U.S.	8.82	7.99	2.94	9.08
Wives' English Proficiency	2.0	1.92	1.78	3.13
Husbands' English Proficiency	2.69	1.50	2.11	3.44
Wives' Satisfaction with Immigration	3.25	4.25	4.09	3.95
Husbands' Satisfaction with Immigration	3.75	4.33	3.76	3.65

Groups one and two were found to be less acculturated than groups three and four. Linear models with wives' and husbands' acculturation as the outcome variable and the

Results

four groups as independent variables were performed. Both regressions for wives' acculturation (F=11.65, p= .0001) and husbands' acculturation (F=12.62, p= .0001) were significant showing that the groups differ in regard to their total acculturation score. Ryan-Einot-Gabriel-Welsch multiple range test of means was conducted to compare the means of the four groups in regard to acculturation. No significant difference between the groups was found, although groups three and four show significantly higher acculturation means than groups one and two for both husbands and wives of each group.

In regard to time in the U.S., groups one, two and four have been longer in the U.S. compared to group three. Time in the U.S. was regressed on the four groups for both wives and husbands. Both regressions for wives' time in the U.S. (F= 15.79, p=.0001) and husbands' time in the U.S. (F=19.68, p=0001) were significant. Through the Ryan-Einot-Gabriel-Welsch multiple range test of means it was found that group three significantly differs from the other groups.

Groups were formed also through language proficiency, which was regressed on the four clusters. Significance was obtained for both English proficiency of the wives (F=6.21, p=.001) and the husbands (F=10.51, p=.001). Ryan-Einot-Gabriel-Welch multiple range test for the wives showed group four as having a significantly higher mean in English proficiency than the other three groups that were not significantly different from each other. Husbands from group four also had a significantly higher English proficiency mean than group two. Groups one, two and three were not significantly different and groups one, three and four were also not found to be significantly different.

Satisfaction with immigration, an aspect of the sample's acculturation, was also entered to form the cluster grouping. A linear regression was performed with satisfaction with immigration as the outcome variable and the four groups as the independent variables showing that the model was significant (F=4.83, p=.005). A Ryan-Einot-Gabriel-Welch multiple range test indicated that husband's group two was significantly higher than the other three groups and that for the wives group two had a significant higher immigration satisfaction than group one.

In summary, the cluster analysis of the fifty couples using Ward's minimum variance criterion based on their acculturation variables (acculturation sum of scores, time in U.S., English language proficiency and satisfaction with immigration) and the Ryan-Einot-Gabriel-Welsch multiple range test of means indicate the following: groups three and four are more acculturated than groups one and two; further, group three despite being more acculturated, had been in the U.S. less time than the other three groups. Moreover, husbands of group four have higher English proficiency than husbands of the other groups. Wives of group four have significantly higher English proficiency compared to wives of group two. Husbands of group two are more satisfied with immigration than the husbands of the other groups. Wives of group two are more satisfied with immigration than wives of group one.

Further, linear models were performed with marital satisfaction, child care, feminine and masculine household task, and gender role attitudes for each spouse, as the outcome variables with the four cluster analysis groups. Table 8 indicates the means of the mentioned variables for each group.

Results

Table 8
Mean of Cluster Groups of Couples on Their Marital Satisfaction, Household, Childcare, Feminine Tasks, Masculine Tasks

Variable	Group 1	Group 2	Group 3	Group 4
N	13	12	9	16
Wives' Marital Satisfaction	98.69	100	109	105
Husband's Marital Satisfaction	109.46	109.1	109	102
Childcare by Wives	.79	.76	.78	.74
Childcare by Husbands	.37	.44	.58	.52
Feminine tasks by Wives	.73	.71	.72	.72
Feminine tasks by Husbands	.32	.41	.41	.35
Masculine tasks by Wives	.18	.27	.23	.26
Masculine tasks by Husbands	.81	.76	.76	.81
Gender role attitudes by Wives	37.8	37.7	42	40.3
Gender role attitudes by Husbands	34.8	33	35	36.9

Simple linear regressions were performed for the four groups with marital satisfaction as the outcome. Non significant values were obtained both for wives (F=.72, p=.54)) and husbands (F=.92, p=.44). No differences among the groups were found through the Ryan-Einot-Gabriel-Welsch multiple range test for the construct marital satisfaction.

The model for the childcare task performed by husbands was significant (F=3.34, p=.027) and accounted for 18% of the variance. Further, Ryan-Einot-Gabriel-Welsch multiple range test of means was conducted to compare the means of the four groups in regard to childcare by husbands. Groups one and three were found to be different. The husbands of group three are more involved with care of their children than husbands of group one as can be seen by their means. As described above, husbands from group one are among the less acculturated than those of group three, although husbands of group one are among the groups that have been longer in the U.S. compared to husbands of group three. In regard to English proficiency the groups were not significantly different.

Linear models with performance of feminine household tasks as outcome variables for the four groups, both for wives and husbands, were conducted. Neither the regression with wives (F=.05, p=.98) nor the regression with husbands (F= 1.47, p=.23) were significant. Further, Ryan-Einot-Gabriel-Welsch multiple range test indicated the groups did not differ significantly from each other.

Performance of masculine household tasks was regressed for husbands and wives for the four groups but was non-significant for wives' groups (F=.68, p=.57) as well as for husbands' groups (F=.31, p=.82) and no mean differences were found among the groups through the Ryan-Einot-Gabriel-Welsch multiple range test.

Gender role attitudes was regressed on the four groups but neither for wives (F=1.13, p=.35) nor for husbands (F=.86, p=.47) was it found to be significant. Ryan-Einot-

Gabriel-Welsch indicated that there were no significant differences among group means.

Qualitative Results

In response to open ended questions regarding the immigration impact on the family or on the couple forty percent of the present sample (n=100) spontaneously mentioned the changes that women go through once in the U.S.. All comments referred to women becoming more independent and more self-assured, as well as taking more initiative. The comment that many marriages between Brazilians had ended in separation was also frequent and associated to the change in the woman's role. The host country was mentioned as a society in which women received a different treatment from that of the country of origin. As two of the husbands' answers and one of the wives illustrate:

> Here in the United States she gains freedom to work ... She feels, as all that this country is, a totally liberal country, she sees herself, the woman, really, talks louder and goes and fights for her rights... she has her rights, she does not accept, some times, what the husband did to her in Brazil (João).

> Here the woman is her own boss. She doesn't need to respect the husband. She doesn't need to talk to anyone. ... So it happens a lot here: women leave, they come here and they want to be like the American women ... And in Brazil, the woman, she has to hold back because, ... because in Brazil she has a duty towards friends, society .... (Paulo).

> If the woman starts to own more, automatically she is going to express her opinion more, from coming repressed, from a country where she felt like that... (Márcia).

Interestingly, the way men behave in relation to women is highlighted by a comment one of the husbands made when answering the acculturation scale. He mentioned the cultural differences between the countries and his example to illustrate this was men's street behavior towards women. He says:

> Here we change, you don't whistle and bug the women in the streets any more. Here it is not a habit like in Brazil everybody does that (José).

Moreover, since many Brazilians work in American households as housecleaners, the family for whom they work for becomes a comparative scenario to their own household situation. The behavior of the American husband and wife that they observe contrasts to the one experienced at home, and in their own culture in general. As one of the women says:

> Here, you see the American (man), he helps the woman in household tasks. The woman arrives, puts her feet up and he goes to the oven. Now wait for a Brazilian (man) to do that, it is bad, ah? (Ana).

Women's rights, the American law regarding women are frequently mentioned. Some men refer to it as a burden, an invasion of the private family life and others as a conquest on women's side. As one of the male interviewees noted:

Results

Women here, she, besides having the support of the law of the United States, it is actually absurd... And I am in big trouble. The women here gain a big strength and, not that I am sexist, it is not that, but the unbalance begins ... (Antonio).

Two of the husbands interviewed who were married for the second time expressed their disenchantment with their previous wives, who according to them, did not take care of the house and their child as their current wife is doing. They left them because "money went up their heads." One of them openly spoke of the present wife as being not so intelligent as the first one, but home oriented (she was pregnant at the time of the interview). Others realized that the separations were a step toward putting an end to what might have been an abusive relationships. Unfair treatment, that is disrespectful and abusive, is mentioned as something common in the way men treat women in Brazil. One of the husbands says:

Because they arrive here and get a job and have conditions to sustain their children, so why is she going to tolerate a man, maybe the husband was not worth or abused her, right? (Pedro).

The qualitative results indicate that the shift in the women's role as they start to work, sometimes gaining a larger wage than their husbands, affects the marital relationship in immigrant Latin couples (Guendelman, 1987; Staples & Mirande, 1980; Rogler, Cortes & Magaldy, 1991) as also suggested in previous studies with Brazilian families (DeBiaggi, 1992, 1996). However, it seems that it is not only the fact of women starting to work that generates a break in the previous gender role concepts of the family, but also the information gathered in the new environment. The observation of American women's and men's behavior, the contact with the law and a society where there has been in general a faster cultural transformation towards women's rights compared to Brazil, provides a favorable context towards change.

CHAPTER 6
Discussion

This chapter discusses the findings of the present research on the acculturation and gender roles of Brazilian immigrant families, as well as how they affect the couples' marital satisfaction. Findings both from the quantitative and the qualitative data will be addressed, with the intent of presenting a more holistic view of the sample studied.

The research was based on the premise that as Brazilian couples acculturate to North American society changes in their gender roles will take place and affect their marital relationships.

First, Brazilians come from a patriarchal society. Compared to the North American one (also patriarchal) it presents more traditional gender roles, as described in chapter one. Thus, Brazilian immigrants bring with them a system of meanings regarding gender role norms acquired in their previous environment. As many researchers indicate, despite regional and social class differences, women and men in Brazil are still largely regarded as responsible for separate spheres in life (Bonamigo & Rasche, 1988; Hahner, 1984; Sarti, 1989; Scott, 1990). Women's primary duty concerns the house and children whereas men are responsible for financially supporting the family. Further, Brazilians come from a society in which women's rights lag behind what has been accomplished in the U.S., except for maternity leave (in Brazil female workers have four moths of paid maternity leave). Legally speaking, women were emancipated only in 1962 (until then they were at the same level as savages, spendthrifts and pubescent minors) and were not considered collaborators in the family responsibilities until 1988. Only with the 1988 constitution the previous concept of head of family household changed, establishing the rights and duties of spouses in an equal basis (Bucher & D'Amorim, 1993).

Second, immigration leads to contact with a distinct cultural milieu and a process of cultural change or acculturation (Berry et al., 1987; Danzinger, 1974; Mena et al., 1987; Padilla et. al., 1985; Phinney et. al., 1992). Thus, it was expected that as Brazilians acculturated, their value system in regard to their previous gender role beliefs and behaviors would undergo a transformation. Studies between acculturation and gender roles with other immigrant populations, on an individual level, have found that acculturation is associated with a liberalization of gender roles (Ghaffarian, 1987; Hannassab, 1991; Torres-Matrullo, 1976, 1980). Other research addressing immigrant families indicates that the move to the U.S. brings the disruption of a past traditional family structure (Guendelman, 1987; Hondagneu-Sotello, 1994; Parrillo, 1991; Pessar, 1984; Queralt, 1984; Staples and Mirande, 1980) and dissatisfaction with men's sustaining a traditional role leads to marital dissolution (Guendelman, 1987; Parrillo, 1991). Similar findings were obtained in a qualitative study with Brazilian immigrant families (DeBiaggi, 1992). As a result of immigrant women's double shift (causing considerable stress and role strain), a

Discussion

high rate of divorce among the immigrant population is also reported (Queralt, 1984; Parrillo, 1991).

Third, American researchers indicate the relationship between gender role attitudes and the domestic division of labor between spouses (Gunter & Gunter, 1990; Hochschild, 1990). Moreover, differing gender role attitudes among spouses and inequalities in the division of household labor have been linked to couple's marital dissatisfaction (Benin & Agostinelli, 1988; Bowen & Orthner, 1983; Hochschild, 1990; Lye & Birblarz, 1993). Thus, Brazilian immigrant's marital quality was expected to be affected by spouses' gender roles (attitudes and behaviors) and acculturation.

It was found that the acculturation (language use, media, ethnic social relations, food preference, ethnic identity) of Brazilians increases as their proficiency in English increases. However, their length of stay in the U.S. has no relation to how acculturated they are. Contrary to the findings of Marin, Otero-Sabogal and Perez-Stable (1987) with Hispanics, time in the U.S. for Brazilians was not associated with a cultural change. It may be that language is a crucial factor in the acculturation process to the new environment. Cultural changes would probably not take place for the Brazilian immigrants if they spoke only their mother tongue, even if they stayed in the United States for many years. Studies could address this interesting matter in order to further investigate the relation of second language acquisition and acculturation.

The results of this research also indicates that acculturation is related to gender role changes in immigrants. In the present study it was found that men's acculturation was related to changing gender role attitudes toward women and men's roles. As the Brazilian male sample acculturated they showed less traditional gender role attitudes. The women, however, did not demonstrate the same association, since no relation between their acculturation and liberalism was found. Thus, the findings partially supported the hypothesis that as the sample became more acculturated they would show less traditional attitudes. Such findings are similar to Torres-Matrullo's (1980) study with Puerto Rican men who changed their attitudes as they acculturated. They do not, however, correspond to findings in the case of Iranian women, for whom acculturation was related to an increase in more liberal attitudes towards gender roles (Hannassab, 1991).

The present study's findings also contradict in part Hondagneu-Sotelo's (1994), whose study with Mexican immigrants did not support the model relating acculturation to gender role changes. She contends that gender role transformation occurs as a function of the immigration and settlement experiences of immigrant families, as well as economic resources. According to Hondagneu-Sotelo, Mexicans live isolated from Americans in immigrant communities, so that an American influence therefore does not make sense. The Brazilian sample's characteristics are quite different from those of the Mexican sample. For instance, many Brazilians are in closer contact with American families through the housecleaning work they perform for them. Both men and women in my sample made frequent comments about the behavior of the American families for whom they worked. Their observations of the American family households and interactions with the family members were vividly described showing the strong impact such experiences have on the immigrants. Historical links between the countries might also be

Discussion

another differential factor. Mexicans have been a longer time in the United States and many have a clear notion of the fact that part of what today is the host country used to belong to Mexico. Brazilians, on the other hand, in general look up to Americans (Martes, 1998) despite past political historical facts between the U.S. and Brazil of which very few have knowledge. As Skidmore, (1988) says, "the U.S. government was another enthusiastic supporter of the coup" that settled military dictatorship in Brazil for twenty-one years. Further, as the results indicate, Brazilians demonstrate a tendency towards an acculturation pattern in which aspects of both cultures are valued, which might account for their openness towards the novel culture, while at the same time maintaining their own cultural characteristics.

The hypothesis that the more acculturated the wives are, the more they will be dissatisfied with their husband's percentage of housework was not supported. Wives' level of acculturation was not associated with satisfaction or dissatisfaction with their husbands' involvement in helping around the house.

However, as husbands acculturated, they did share more childcare with their wives. This finding partially supported what was expected, that is, that husbands that share more childcare and housework are more acculturated and have more liberal gender role attitudes. Husband's acculturation was associated to their gender role attitude change towards a more liberal view and greater involvement with their children. One of the husbands exemplifies such transformation when mentioning his change after having answered the household and childcare task questions:

Husband: The task here is all divided but there (in Brazil) she did 70% or more. Life abroad teaches us a lot, and if by any chance we go back I already know how it is. That, that Brazilian machismo I think is a disease, I learned that here. It has to be cut, it has to be cured...
Researcher: But there are people who do not think like you?
Husband: Many, many, still, right? But some already do, around us.

The hypothesis that marital adjustment would be higher for wife and husband when both had similar gender role attitudes than when they had dissimilar gender role attitudes was not supported. Having similar or dissimilar gender role attitudes was not associated to their marital quality, which is different from what has been indicated by some studies with American samples (Bowen and Orthner, 1983; Lye and Birblaz, 1993). Perhaps the present findings indicate the complexity of the matter. It might be that looking only at gender role attitude congruency does not explain marital quality especially when addressing immigrant families.

In fact, it was found that marital satisfaction could be predicted by the level of spouse's acculturation and gender role, as expected. Brazilian wives' marital satisfaction was higher as a result of the gender role attitudes and acculturation of both spouses, and particularly of their husbands' gender role attitudes and acculturation. However, for the wives of less acculturated husbands, when their spouses became more liberal wives' marital satisfaction increased. In contrast, when husbands were more acculturated their liberalism was related to lower satisfaction among wives. Perhaps the husbands' increase

Discussion

in acculturation and gender role attitudes presents a shift in their previous relational pattern bringing other issues to the marital relation that could be somewhat more complex. Wives' expectations of the marital relationship may be higher for the more acculturated group. It might be that wives expect their husbands to be more expressive in their relationship.

The husband's marital satisfaction, on the other hand, was not determined by any of these factors, although there is evidence that the performance of feminine household tasks contributed to their marital satisfaction. Thus, husbands who were involved with feminine household labor were better adjusted in their conjugal relationship. An increase in the wives' marital satisfaction was also related to their husbands' involvement in taking care of their children. Similar findings were obtained by Hochschild (1989), who indicated that couples where the husband performed more household and childcare were more satisfied in their marital relationship. In Hochschild's study, the husbands who shared more household work were also more satisfied. An example of a Brazilian wife, whose husband now shares household tasks and childcare with her, illustrates the husband's greater involvement and as a result an improvement in their relationship:

> Wife: He didn't understand why I was tired. I worked, I cleaned houses, I took S. to the soccer game, to the babysitter, I did the groceries, I did everything and he used to ask: Why are you tired? But when we started to work together he started to see that my work was as heavy as his was, and he started to participate because we worked together. We took S. together to the babysitter. He started to go to soccer practice. He

started to watch the game. He started to participate more in S.'s life, right? So things got better.
Researcher: How was it in Brazil?
Wife: In Brazil it is very common for the woman to take care of the house and the husband to go to the bar and drink beer, isn't it? ... it is a matter of culture. Not here, here you see the American man, the husband after dinner, they have dishwasher, all right, but he is the one to put the plates in the dishwasher. It is his job.

Findings for the hypothesis that wives would be more liberal in their gender roles a shorter period of time since their arrival than would husbands were in part supported. Women with a shorter period of time in the U.S. were more liberal than men who were here for the same amount of time. However, wives had a more liberal gender role attitude than husbands regardless of how long they had been in the new country. A relation was found between time in the U.S. and more liberal attitudes towards gender roles for the husbands. But even when they become more liberal they were still not as liberal as the women. Such findings add to other studies that found that women have more liberal gender role attitudes than men (Spence &Hahn, 1997; Peplau & Gordon, 1985; Twenge, 1997).

Further, as indicated by the qualitative results, for many Brazilian women the perception of their oppressive position in their culture of origin might be latent, only waiting for a different context in order to emerge, as in a society where questioning of the previous status quo is more acceptable. That supposition can be illustrated by a wife's comment in response to the researcher's question about her opinion on the questionnaire:

Discussion

Wife: I liked these questions, when it got to this part [Gender role attitudes measure] because I hate that of people thinking that men have to be this or that, that the male child has to be more. ... I like women's freedom very much, I think every woman has to be free...

Researcher: Before you came you didn't work, right, how was that?

Wife: It was terrible, terrible because during my whole life I had this drive, the drive spoke louder, of gaining my own money of not depending on anybody. Because all my life, I am from a small town where you have to ask your father's permission to go to the movies, I had to ask for money, it depended on his will. To go to a party the brother had to go together. And that never worked very well in my head, never, I thought that the responsibility was mine. ... So, when I married, my husband had that idea because it is something that goes from father to son in Brazil, I don't know: the woman doesn't work, the woman doesn't work. So we always had arguments, poor women are the ones that don't work because rich women work. It is the wife of the poor that doesn't work. I never accepted that. ... So I think and am raising my daughter to make her financial freedom and never get married because in Brazil exists that way: the young woman has to marry because her mother is terrified that she will stay at home, I think it is absurd. Is very scared, has to marry, has to marry. The woman marries to wash dishes to do this and that and never has liberty and my daughter I say to her, the day you get married you marry for love you don't need to, don't think like people think in Brazil, don't marry because of situation, no. Marry for situation because the father can't stand any longer, this and that, the fear. So today I think much better, he fixed 100% because if he had that machismo, in his head, I wouldn't live. So to speak, it got fixed, it is normal for him to help me at home, there is none of that confusion, you understand? ... So here was very good for me because I had that since I was little, when I was raised by my father.

It might be argued that for men the environment is a factor related to their change towards less traditionalism, as indicated also by an association of acculturation and gender role attitudes. Further, the frequent comments regarding the greater women's rights in the U.S. and the legal penalties for batterers, as well as the perception of the different behaviors of Americans, had an impact on them. The cultural milieu in their case promotes their change. But for women, as other researchers have suggested, (Morokvasic, Hondagneu-Sotello, 1994) change in their gender roles is not merely resultant of the new environment, but have past and present influences. The perception of their past experiences and the possibility to act on them in the present seem to be intertwined. If they had moved to another country as sexist as Brazil or even more, they would probably not have experienced the transformation they went through.

Whether or not this is due to an "Americanization" seems to be a more complex issue than merely considering acculturation as the dominant group's influence on a minority group. In the present study, the finding that acculturation is related to the men's transformation towards greater liberalism might attest to the importance of women's achievements in the fight for their rights, which have without any doubt been greater in the U.S. than in Brazil. As Morokvasic says, "sexist oppression and subordination experienced by women in different parts of

Discussion

the world are not an individual matter, nor a matter of specific personal relationships that concern some individuals exceptionally" (1984, p. 899).

The present findings connote some clinical implications. It has been shown that acculturation has an impact on immigrant families. This study particularly addresses the relationships of immigrant couples and how acculturation and changes in gender role attitudes and behavior affect the quality of the marital relationship. Although in a research study factors are mentioned in a very abstract way, we have to keep in mind that each of the constructs addressed correspond to important aspects in people's lives. Immigrants come from a different social system where cultural values and orientations guided their beliefs, behaviors, and conceptualizations of what women and men should do, feel or think. The broader socio-cultural environment influenced also the organizational pattern of the family (Anderson and Sabatelli, 1995). Thus, clinicians, when seeing immigrant patients, should bear in mind that individuals coming from a distinct milieu bring with them an understanding of themselves and others according to their previous socio-cultural reality. The transformations that take place with acculturation and contact with the new culture bring changes to their most intimate relationships. Many feel as if they have lost ground. Men and women many times feel and believe they are losing their masculinity and femininity because of changes in their past attitudes and behaviors in regard to their gender roles or they feel their partner is no longer acting as previously required and thus not being a man or a women any longer. Thus tensions arise. As Gilbert (1985) reminds us, conflicts in this area involve a deep-rooted value system within each family member. Therefore, practitioners or any other professional working with immigrant families need to recognize the internal struggle that immigration implies for each family and individual.

Brazilian immigrant families come to add to the Latin immigrant population in the U.S. As many have pointed out (Anderson and Sabatelli, 1995), many differences exist within groups that are many times considered as one in the U.S., such as Hispanics that include people from a variety of countries from Central and South America (Brazilians by the way are not Hispanics). However, Latin cultures do share the value of familism, that is, family includes not only nuclear but extended family and a strong bond and sense of loyalty is felt between members of that group. Likewise, Brazilians have a strong sense of affiliation to the family group which provides in turn a sense of protection and caring (DeBiaggi, 1992). But as traditional gender roles imply, women are the ones identified with maintaining the unity of the family. Thus, as other studies with immigrants have indicated (Guendelman, 1987; Rogler, Cortes & Magaldy, 1991), when there is a change in women's past role, many of their husbands see that as a threat to family unity and care.

It should be highlighted here that gender role changes do not necessarily mean a change in the extremely valuable, humane and important familism existent in Latin cultures. Gender role changes can mean a break in the family if both the husband and the wife do not share the responsibility of caring for the family members in the Latin way. The families in which the fathers are more involved with their children and satisfied with the enrichment of their role indicate that caring for the members of the nuclear and extended family can only bring warmth to both women and men and keep familism as important as it should be.

Discussion

Further exploration is needed to learn more about the family experience in the immigration process. This study was limited to nuclear families and looked at the relationship between the couples' gender roles, acculturation and marital satisfaction. Other studies might address gender roles and acculturation between members of first and second generation or between different types of families. Moreover, there are many other dimensions that this study did not consider such as sexuality, political values and the role of religious institutions within the family. Replication of the present study requires that a bilingual researcher be present at every interview, since as mentioned in chapter two, this population is not used to responding to fixed-response questions. Mailing a questionnaire of such intimate issues would probably be interpreted as a very cold and disrespectful act. As other researchers (Hondagneu-Sotelo, 1994) have noted, the personal contact in the Latin population is highly valued.

In brief, this research provides a conceptual model indicating the importance of acculturation and gender role changes to immigrant couples' marital relationship which may help to frame future studies of immigrant families as well as interventions with immigrant families. Finally, this thesis acknowledges the great effort of every individual family member in this new journey toward a better family life. It is hoped that the examples of greater involvement from fathers and mothers in family life that resulted in greater satisfaction for both, will be a confirmation that changes in gender role patterns can take place and bring more meaningfulness to familial relationships.

Appendix A: Consent Forms

Informed Consent

Dear Sir or Ms

I am a Brazilian graduate student in the psychology department at Boston University. I would like to invite you to take part in a research study that I am conducting of how Brazilian emigrant couples with children view and experience family life in the new country. My work is being supervised by Leslie Brody who is an associate professor in the psychology department.

In order to participate you would have to be available for about a one hour interview each with me. I will ask you questions about yourself (like for instance, what was your job in Brazil and what language do you speak most) and questions about you and your spouse (for instance, how you organize family life). The interview will be recorded but as soon as I have transcribed it the tapes will be erased. All of your answers will remain completely confidential, that is, unless you wish, no one will know who has answered these questions. You and your spouse are invited to participate. The interview, however, is done individually and I ask that before finishing both interviews you do not share information about it with each other.

By participating you will have the opportunity of thinking about some issues related to your life in the new country with your spouse and family. You will also be contributing to our knowledge of how immigration affects Brazilian families and how we can assist them when necessary. Further, you will have the opportunity of learning how other couples experience and view the same issues, since you can ask to be sent an overall research results. In addition, I wish to demonstrate my appreciation of your participation by offering you a gift certificate of $20 for a Brazilian restaurant or a Brazilian ethnic store in your area of residence to each couple's complete interview.

If at any time during the interview you wish to interrupt and discontinue the interview process you may do so without concern. Further, you are free not to answer any question that you do not feel comfortable answering. If you have any other questions regarding the research or my person please contact me at the below address.

If you agree to participate in this research please sign the paragraph that follows.

Sincerely,

Sylvia Dantas DeBiaggi, MA
64 Cummington Street
Boston University
Boston, MA 02215
Contact Phone: (617) 776-4034

Appendix B

Having read the informed consent letter about the research described above, I am aware that my participation is on a voluntary basis. I understand that I am free to ask questions, express my concerns and refuse to answer any item or interrupt my participation in the research at any time. I will communicate Sylvia Dantas DeBiaggi personally or through the telephone (617) 776-4034 any question or difficulty in relation to the research.

I have received a copy of the informed consent.

Signature of participant:_____

Date:_____

Please note: If you are interested in receiving a summary of the overall results by mail, I need to be able to reach you by mail. In case you are interested, please provide your name and address below.

This sheet will remain separate from your questionnaire. It will not be linked to your answers at any time, and it will be destroyed after I mail you the results.

Therefore, I am providing my name and address for mailing purposes only:

Name:_____

Address:_____

Appendix B: Questionnaire

Questionnaire

Date of interview___/___/___   Number:_____

1) Date of Birth: ___/___/_____   2) Sex:_____
               Day Month Year

3) City and state of residence before leaving Brazil:_____

4) City and state of birth:_____

5) Marital status:
                    a) single
                    b) married
                    c) divorced
                    d) separated
                    e) widow/widower
                    f) common law union

6) Date of marriage (or when you started to live together): ___/___/___
                                                                         day month year

7) This is your _____ marriage or common law union.
            (1st, 2nd, 3rd, etc)

8) How many children?____   sex:_____   DOB:_____
                                            sex:_____   DOB:_____
                                            sex:_____   DOB:_____
                                            sex:_____   DOB:_____

9) Highest level of education completed_____

10) Do you work ? (Please give job titles or duties)
_____

If unemployed, what was your last job?_____

11) How many hours do(did) you work per week? _____

12) How much do you earn (earned) per week?_____

13) Did you work in Brazil? (Please give job titles or duties of last job):
_____

14) How many hours did you work per week in Brazil ?_____

15) Current Religion:_____

16) When did you arrive in the USA.?   _____/_____
                                                          month   year

17) Do you wish to go back to Brazil?
        a) Yes
        b) No

18) You consider your present family life:
        a) better than it was in Brazil
        b) somewhat better than it was in Brazil
        c) the same as it was in Brazil
        d) somewhat worse than it was in Brazil
        e) worse than it was in Brazil

19) If you had to, would you immigrate to the U.S. again? Would you do it all over again?
        a) definitely not
        b) maybe not
        c) not sure
        d) maybe yes
        e) definitely yes

Appendix B

20) Are you sorry you came?
    a) definitely sorry
    b) moderately sorry
    c) somewhat sorry
    d) slightly sorry
    e) definitely not sorry

21) How happy are you that you came?
    a) not at all happy
    b) a little happy
    c) somewhat happy
    d) happy
    e) extremely happy

Probe questions:

In relation to your feelings about coming here:

A. Do you think the way you are feeling has affected the way your family is functioning?

B. How much of the way you are feeling is a consequence of how your family is functioning?

22) Would you recommend immigrating to the U.S. to other Brazilian families in the same situation as yours?
    a) definitely not
    a) maybe not
    b) not sure
    c) maybe
    d) definitely

A. What would you tell them the way that immigration affects the family (positive and/or negative aspects)?

B. What would you tell them in regard to how immigration affects the relationship with spouse (husband or wife/ positive and negative aspects)?

23) Are you feeling the way you imagined you would before coming to the U.S.? How does your present situation compare to what you expected it would be?

        a) very disappointed
        b) disappointed
        c) disappointed with some things but also better with others
        d) better
        e) much better than thought before

Acculturation Scale

The following questions are about cultural aspects of your life. Please indicate below your choice of option.

1) The persons you visit or who visit you are:

All Brazilians	More Brazilians than Americans	About Half & Half	More Americans than Brazilians	All Americans
___	___	___	___	___

2) You prefer going to social gatherings/parties at which the people are:

All Brazilians	More Brazilians than Americans	About Half & Half	More Americans than Brazilians	All Americans
___	___	___	___	___

3) Your close friends are:

All Brazilians	More Brazilians than Americans	About Half & Half	More Americans than Brazilians	All Americans
___	___	___	___	___

Appendix B

4) If you had the choice, would you want your children's friends to be:

___	___	___	___	___
All Brazilians	More Brazilians than Americans	About Half & Half	More Americans than Brazilians	All Americans

5) If you could choose the ethnicity of your neighborhood you would want your neighbors to be:

___	___	___	___	___
All Brazilians	More Brazilians than Americans	About Half & Half	More Americans than Brazilians	All Americans

6) In general, what language(s) do you read?

___	___	___	___	___
Only Portuguese	More Portuguese than English	Both equally	More English than Portuguese	Only English

7) In which language(s) do you usually think?

___	___	___	___	___
Only Portuguese	More Portuguese than English	Both equally	More English than Portuguese	Only English

8) What language(s) do you usually speak with coworkers?

___	___	___	___	___
Only Portuguese	More Portuguese than English	Both equally	More English than Portuguese	Only English

9) What language(s) do you usually speak with your friends?

___	___	___	___	___
Only Portuguese	More Portuguese than English	Both equally	More English than Portuguese	Only English

10) What language(s) you usually speak with your spouse?

Only Portuguese	More Portuguese than English	Both equally	More English than Portuguese	Only English
___	___	___	___	___

11) What language(s) do you usually speak with your children?

Only Portuguese	More Portuguese than English	Both equally	More English than Portuguese	Only English
___	___	___	___	___

12) In general, in what language(s) are the radio programs you listen to?

Only Portuguese	More Portuguese than English	Both equally	More English than Portuguese	Only English
___	___	___	___	___

13) In general, in what language(s) are the TV programs you watch?

Only Portuguese	More Portuguese than English	Both equally	More English than Portuguese	Only English
___	___	___	___	___

14) In general, in what language(s) are the video film and programs you watch?

Only Portuguese	More Portuguese than English	Both equally	More English than Portuguese	Only English
___	___	___	___	___

15) In general, in what language(s) are the movies, TV, videos and radio programs you prefer to watch and listen to?

Only Portuguese	More Portuguese than English	Both equally	More English than Portuguese	Only English
___	___	___	___	___

Appendix B

16) You prefer to eat:

| Only Brazilian food | More Brazilian than American food | Half & Half | More American than Brazilian food | Only American food |

17) How do you consider yourself?

| Very Brazilian | More Brazilian than American | Half & Half | More American than Brazilian | Very American |

Household and Childcare Tasks

Now I am going to ask you about house duties and childcare. These same questions will be asked to many other couples and in that way we might know more about how families organize their home life.

Please indicate how much each of you does the following tasks at home. You will fill in a circle according to how much each does the task. The circle is divided in ten parts.

For instance, if your partner frequently writes letters to relatives you are going to fill many parts of the circle for him/her, if you write some you will fill out a few parts for you. Suppose that you and your partner write New Year's cards together, fill out a part for the joint activity.

Use [color] to indicate your partner and [color] to indicate your part. Use [color] to indicate when you do the task together. If there is a third person other than you and your spouse who lives with you or spends at least three days per week (e.g.: grandparent or child care helper) use [color]. Please note the person's sex, age and relation to your family_____

The whole circle should be filled.

Example:
Writes letters to relatives

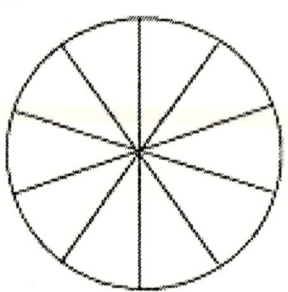

1. Takes child to birthday parties

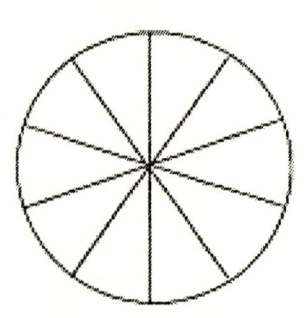

2. Takes child to doctor/dentist

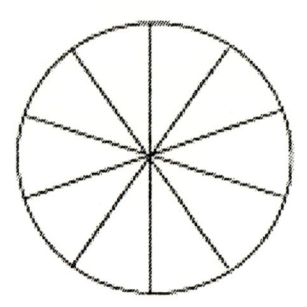

Appendix B

3. Goes to teacher conferences

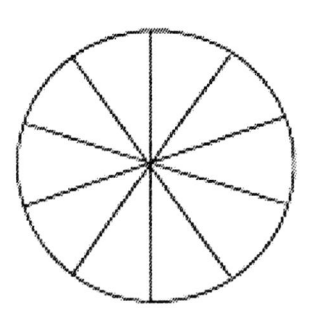

4. Supervises child's morning routine

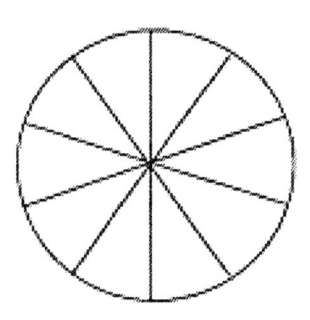

5. Puts child to bed

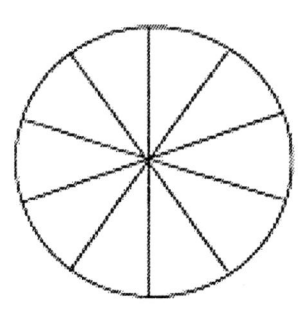

6. Takes child to or from lessons (school, daycare)

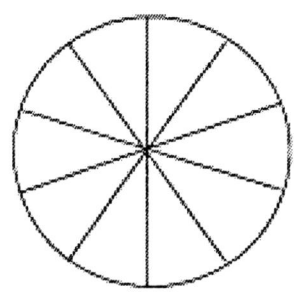

7. Buys child's clothes

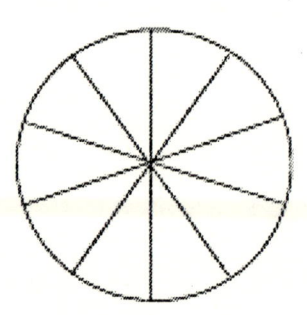

8. Takes child on outings

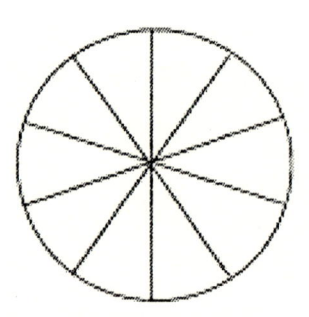

9. Makes childcare/babysitting arrangements

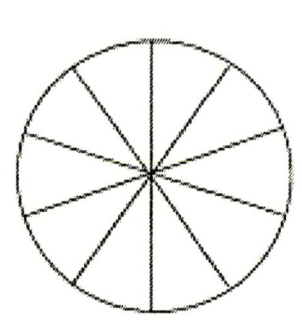

10. Disciplines

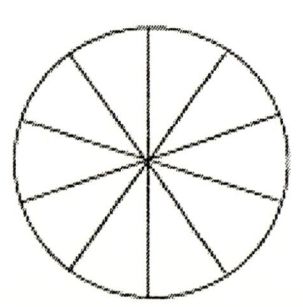

Appendix B 127

11. Helping with homework

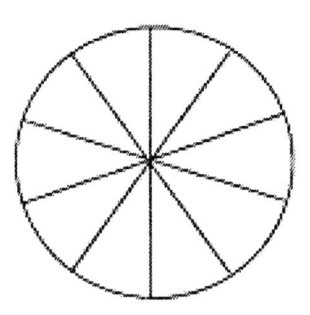

12. Stays with sick child, or makes arrangements for care when child is sick

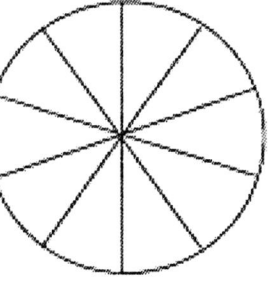

13. Supervises child's hygiene such as baths, brushing teeth, etc.

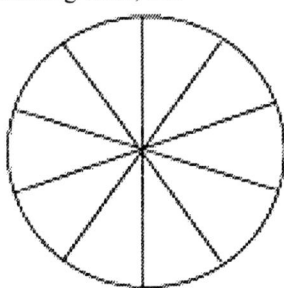

14. Plays with child

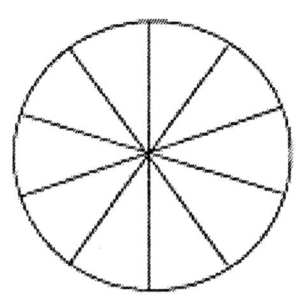

15. Goes to school events such as plays, expositions

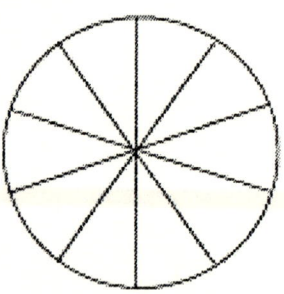

16. Cleans the house

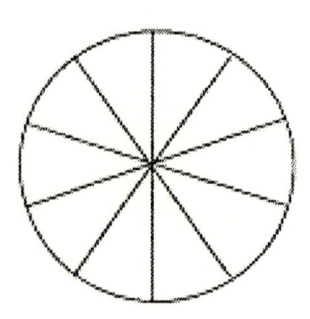

17. Car maintenance and repairs

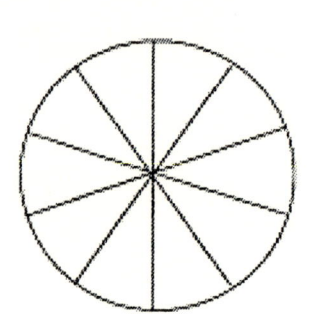

18. Pays bills

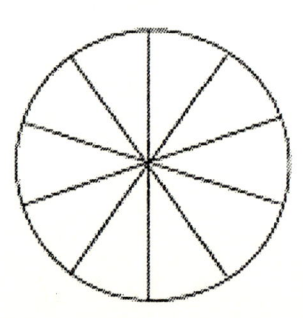

Appendix B

19. Yard work

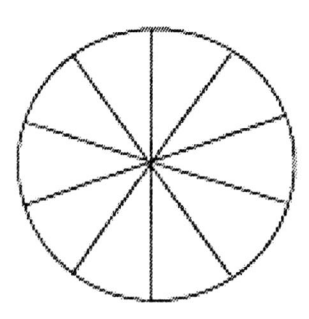

20. Meal preparation

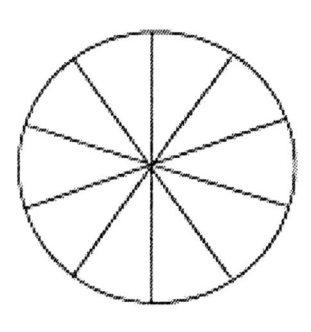

21. Laundry

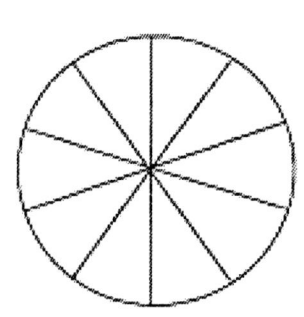

22. Folds and puts away washed clothes

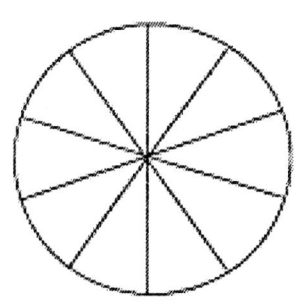

23. Grocery shopping

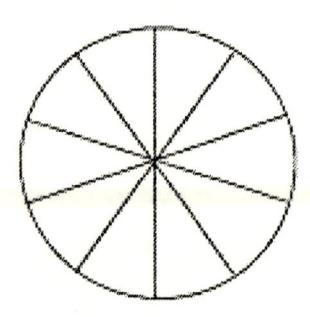

24. Organizing social life

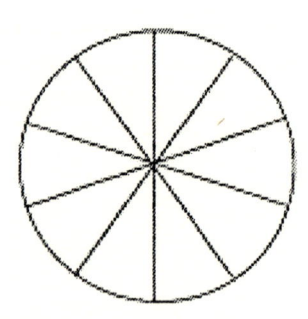

25. Meal clean-up

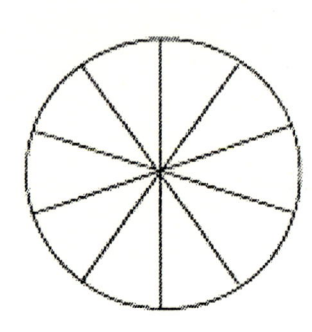

26. Makes the bed

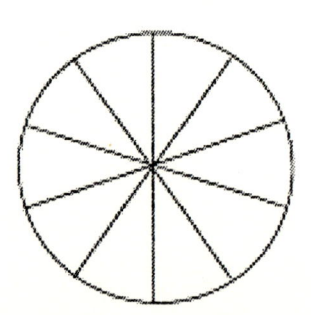

Appendix B 131

27. Takes the garbage out

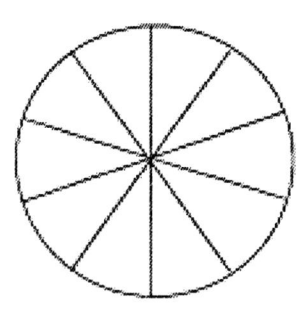

28. Household repairs

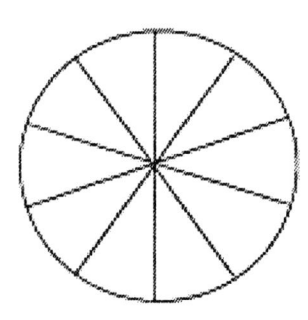

29. Takes care of houseplants

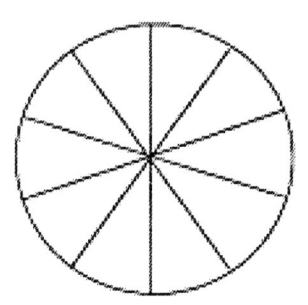

30. How satisfied are you with the way you and your spouse are dividing up household tasks and childcare?

1=extremely satisfied
2=very satisfied
3=somewhat satisfied
4=neither satisfied nor unsatisfied
5=somewhat unsatisfied
6=very unsatisfied
7=extremely unsatisfied

If you could change something(s) about the way you and your spouse divide up household tasks and childcare, what would you change?

_____

Dyadic Adjustment

Now you are going to read or hear questions about your relationship with your husband (wife). These same questions are going to be asked to many other couples. In that way we may know how other people deal with matters or problems that are common to all. Please note that no one will know who answered what, that is, it is confidential. There is no right or wrong answer. Please indicate what happens with you with no fear to be sincere.

Most persons have disagreements in their relationships. Please indicate below the approximate extent of agreement or disagreement between you and your partner for each item on the following list.

	Always agree	Almost always agree	Occasionally disagree	Frequently disagree	Almost always disagree	Always disagree
1. Handling family matters	____	____	____	____	____	____

Appendix B 133

2. Matters of recreation ___ ___ ___ ___ ___ ___

3. Religious matters ___ ___ ___ ___ ___ ___

4. Demonstrations of affection ___ ___ ___ ___ ___ ___

5. Friends ___ ___ ___ ___ ___ ___

6. Conventionality (correct or proper behavior) ___ ___ ___ ___ ___ ___

7. Philosophy of life ___ ___ ___ ___ ___ ___

8. Ways of dealing with parents or in-laws ___ ___ ___ ___ ___ ___

9. Aims, goals, and things believed important ___ ___ ___ ___ ___ ___

10. Amount of time spent together ___ ___ ___ ___ ___ ___

11. Making major decisions ___ ___ ___ ___ ___ ___

12. Household tasks ___ ___ ___ ___ ___ ___

13. Leisure time, interests and activities   _____ _____ _____ _____ _____ _____

14. Career decisions   _____ _____ _____ _____ _____ _____

15. Sex relations   _____ _____ _____ _____ _____ _____

	All the time	Most of the time	More often than not	Occasionally	Rarely	Never
16. How often do you discuss or have you considered divorce, separation, or terminating your relationship?						
17. How often do you or your mate leave the house after a fight?	___	___	___	___	___	___
18. In general, how often do you think that things between you and your partner are going well?	___	___	___	___	___	___
19. Do you confide in your mate?	___	___	___	___	___	___
20. Do you ever regret that you married?(or lived together)	___	___	___	___	___	___
21. How often do you and your partner quarrel?	___	___	___	___	___	___
22. How often do you and your mate "get on each other's nerves?"	___	___	___	___	___	___

Appendix B

	Every day	Almost every day	Occasionally	Rarely	Never
23. Do you kiss your mate?	___	___	___	___	___

	All of them	Most of them	Some of them	Very few of them	None of them
24. Do you and your mate engage in outside interests together?	___	___	___	___	___

How often would you say the following events occur between you and your mate?

	Never	Less than once a month	Once or twice a month	Once or twice a week	Once a day	More often
25. Have a stimulating exchange of ideas	___	___	___	___	___	___
26. Laugh together	___	___	___	___	___	___
27. Calmly discuss something	___	___	___	___	___	___
28. Work together on a project	___	___	___	___	___	___

There are some things about which couples sometimes agree and sometime disagree. Indicate if either item below caused differences of opinions or were problems in your relationship during the past few weeks. (Check yes or no)

	Yes	No	
29.	___	___	Being too tired for Sex
30.	___	___	Not showing love

31. The dots on the following line represent different degrees of happiness in your relationship. The middle point "happy" represents the degree of happiness of most relationships. Please circle the dot which best describes the degree of happiness, all things considered, of your relationship.

*　　*　　*　　*　　*　　*　　*

Extremely unhappy　Fairly unhappy　A little unhappy　Happy　Very happy　Extremely happy　Perfect

32. Which of the following statements best describes how you feel about the future of your relationship?

___ I want desperately for my relationship to succeed and would go to almost any length to see that it does.
___ I want very much for my relationship to succeed, and will do all I can to see that it does.
___ I want very much for my relationship to succeed, and will do my fair share to see that it does.
___ It would be nice if my relationship succeeded, but I can't do much more than I am doing now to help it succeed.
___ It would be nice if my relationship succeeded, but I refuse to do any more than I am doing now to keep the relationship going.
___ My relationship can never succeed, and there is no more that I can do to keep the relationship going.

Appendix B

Attitude Towards Women

Below you will read or listen to different people's statements that describe attitudes toward the roles of women in society. There are no right or wrong answers, only opinions. Please indicate what you feel in relation to what is said by choosing one alternative: agree strongly; agree mildly; disagree mildly; disagree strongly

1. Swearing and obscenity are more repulsive in the speech of a woman than a man.

   _____ Agree strongly   _____ Agree mildly   _____ Disagree mildly   _____ Disagree strongly

2. Under modern economic conditions with woman being active outside the home, men should share in household tasks such as washing dishes and doing the laundry.

   _____ Agree strongly   _____ Agree mildly   _____ Disagree mildly   _____ Disagree strongly

3. It is insulting to women to have the "obey" clause remain in the marriage service.

   _____ Agree strongly   _____ Agree mildly   _____ Disagree mildly   _____ Disagree strongly

4. A woman should be free as a man to propose marriage.

   _____ Agree strongly   _____ Agree mildly   _____ Disagree mildly   _____ Disagree strongly

5. Women should worry less about their rights and more about becoming good wives and mothers.

   _____ Agree strongly   _____ Agree mildly   _____ Disagree mildly   _____ Disagree strongly

6. Women should assume their rightful place in business and all the professions along with men.

_____ Agree strongly   _____ Agree mildly   _____ Disagree mildly   _____ Disagree strongly

7. A woman should not expect to go to exactly the same places or to have quite the same freedom of action as a man.

_____ Agree strongly   _____ Agree mildly   _____ Disagree mildly   _____ Disagree strongly

8. It is ridiculous for a woman to run a locomotive and for a man to darn socks.

_____ Agree strongly   _____ Agree mildly   _____ Disagree mildly   _____ Disagree strongly

9. The intellectual leadership of a community should be largely in the hands of men.

_____ Agree strongly   _____ Agree mildly   _____ Disagree mildly   _____ Disagree strongly

10. Women should be given equal opportunity with men for apprenticeship in the various trades.

_____ Agree strongly   _____ Agree mildly   _____ Disagree mildly   _____ Disagree strongly

11. Women earning as much as their dates should bear equally the expense when they go out together.

_____ Agree strongly   _____ Agree mildly   _____ Disagree mildly   _____ Disagree strongly

12. Sons in a family should be given more encouragement to go to college than daughters.

_____ Agree strongly   _____ Agree mildly   _____ Disagree mildly   _____ Disagree strongly

Appendix B

13. In general, the father should have greater authority than the mother in the bringing up of children.

_____ Agree strongly _____ Agree mildly _____ Disagree mildly _____ Disagree strongly

14. Economic and social freedom is worth far more to women than acceptance of the ideal of femininity, which has been set up by men.

_____ Agree strongly _____ Agree mildly _____ Disagree mildly _____ Disagree strongly

15. There are many jobs in which men should be given preference over women in being hired or promoted.

_____ Agree strongly _____ Agree mildly _____ Disagree mildly _____ Disagree strongly

16. I would be more comfortable with a male boss than with a female boss.

_____ Agree strongly _____ Agree mildly _____ Disagree mildly _____ Disagree strongly

17. It is morally wrong for a woman to maintain extramarital relationships but it is not so bad for a man to have them (extramarital relationships).

_____ Agree strongly _____ Agree mildly _____ Disagree mildly _____ Disagree strongly

18. Women's sexual desires are not as strong as men's are.

_____ Agree strongly _____ Agree mildly _____ Disagree mildly _____ Disagree strongly

19. In regard to sex relations men should always take the initiative.

_____ Agree strongly _____ Agree mildly _____ Disagree mildly _____ Disagree strongly

English Language Proficiency

1) How well would you say you speak and understand English at the present time. Please check the column below:

a. No knowledge or understanding of English at all. ___

b. Fluent enough to express elementary needs and to understand simple English (for example, buy stamps at the post office or give simple directions) ___

c. Fluent enough to handle limited work requirements and most social situations ___

d. Fluent enough to participate in most conversations on familiar practical, social, and professional topics (for example, a conversation on Brazilian recipes or a discussion on the quality of TV programs) ___

e. Fluent enough to participate in all conversations on both familiar and unfamiliar topics ___

f. Totally fluent, like a native American ___

References

Almeida, A., Carneiro, M. & Paula, S. (1987). *Pensando a familia no Brasil: Da colônia à modernidade.* Rio de Janeiro: Espaço e Tempo.

Anderson, S. A & Sabatelli, R. M. (1995). *Family Interaction: A Multigenerational Developmental Perspective.* Boston: Allyn and Bacon.

Assis, G. (1995). *Estar aqui, estar lá ... uma cartografia da vida entre dois lugares.* Unpublished Master Thesis, Universidade Federal de Santa Catarina, Florianópolis, Brazil.

Azar, B. (1999, March 3). Wider path to cultural understanding: researchers move toward a multicultural, rather than linear, model of acculturation. *APA Monitor, vol.30*(3).

Azevedo, T. (1963). *Social Change in Brazil.* Gainsville: University of Florida Press.

Barroso, C. L. (1975). A participação da mulher no desenvolvimento científico brasileiro. *Ciência e cultura, 27(6),* 613-620.

Baruch, G.K., & Barnett, R.C (1986). Father's participation in family work and children's sex role attitudes. *Child Development, 5*, 1218-1223.

Bassanezi, M. (1995). Imigrações internacionais no Brasil: um panorama histórico. In Neide Patarra (Ed.) *Emigração e imigração internacionais no Brasil contemporâneo.* Campinas: FNUAP

Brasil continua sendo um país que acolhe muitos estrangeiros (2000, June 18). *O Estado de São Paulo,* p. A18.

Benin M. & Agostinelli, J. (1988). Husband's and wives' satisfaction with the division of labor. *Journal of Marriage and the Family, 50,* 349-361.

Behrman, D.(1982). *Family and /or career: Plans of first-time mothers.* Ann Harbor: UMI Research Press.

Berry, J. (1980). Acculturation as varieties of adaptation. In A. Padilla (ed.) *Acculturation: Theories, models and some findings,* (pp. 9-25). Boulder: Westview Press.

Berry, J., Kim, U., Minde, T. & Mok, D. (1987). Comparative studies of acculturative stress. *International Migration Review, 21(3),* 491-511.

Berry, J., Portinga, Y. , Segal, & Dasen, (1992). *Cross-cultural psychology: Research and applications.* New York: Cambridge University Press.

References

Bicalho, J. (1989). *Yes, eu sou Brazuca, ou a vida do imigrante brasileiro nos Estados Unidos da América*. Governador Valadares: Fundaçao Serviços de Educaçao e Cultura (FUNSEC).

Blake, A. (1989, November 6). Stronger scents of home. *The Boston Globe*, p. 19.

Blay, E. and Conceição, R. (1990). *Mulher, ciência e sociedade: Abordagem das relações de gênero nas disciplinas da universidade de São Paulo*. Trabalho apresentado no primeiro congresso Luso-Afro-Brasileiro de Ciências Sociais, Coimbra, Portugal.

Block, Jeanne H. (1973). Conceptions of sex role. Some cross-cultural and longitudinal perspectives. *American Psychologist, 28*, 512-526.

Bonamigo, E.M. & Rasche, V.M. (1988). O processo de socialização da criança nas famílias de classe popular. *Psicologia: Teoria e pesquisa, 4(3)*, 295-315.

Bowen, G. & Orthner, D. (1983). Sex-role congruency and marital quality. *Journal of Marriage and the Family, 45*, 223-230.

Brody, L. (1993). On understanding gender differences in the expression of emotion. In Ablon, J., Brown, D., Khantzian, E. and Mack, J. (Eds.), *Human feelings. Explorations in Affect Development and Meaning* (pp. 87-121). Hillsdale, NJ: Analytic Press

Brody, L. and Flanagan, L. (1990). *Gender role correlates of fear in women and men*. Paper presented at the American Psychological Association, Obston, MA.

Brody, L. & Hall, J. (1993). Gender and emotion. In M. Lewis & J. Havilland (eds.), *Handbook of emotions*. New York: Guilford Press.

Brooke, J. (1990, November 30). Governador Valadares Journal: You might say this is the town Uncle Sam built. *The New York Times*, p. 4.

Bruschini, C. (1994). O trabalho da mulher no Brasil: Tendências recentes. In H. I. B. Saffioti & M. Munoz-Vargas' (Eds.), *Mulher brasileira é assim* (pp. 63-94). Rio de Janeiro: Rosa dos Tempos.

Bucher J.F. & D'Amorim, M.A. (1993). Brazil. In L. Adler (Ed.), *International handboook on gender roles*. Westport, Connecticut: Greenwood Press.

Calligaris, C. (1999). Desculpem o politicamente incorreto. *Folha de São Paulo*, Pag. Ilustrada, 4-8.

Campbel, J. & Snow, B. (1992). Gender role conflict and family environment as predictors of men's marital satisfaction. *Journal of Family Psychology, 6(1)*, 84-87.

Candido, A. (1951). The Brazilian family. In T.L. Smith & A. Marchant (Eds.), *Brazil: Portrait of half a continent* (pp. 291-312). New York: Dryden Press.

Canzian, F. (1994, July 11). Imigrantes da Copa assustam EUA. *Folha de São Paulo*, Pag. Esporte 4-8,4-9.

References

Canzian, F. (1995, October 19). Brasil-Japão 100 anos. *Folha de São Paulo*, Pag. Especial 2.

Chafetz, J. & Hagan, J. (1996). The gender division of labor and family change in industrial societies: A theoretical accounting. *Journal of Comparative Family Studies, 27 (2)*, pp. 187-219.

Chodorow, N. (1974). Family structure and feminine personality. In M. Rosaldo (Ed.), *Women, culture and society*. California: Stanford University Press.

Chodorow, N. (1978). *The reproduction of mothering: Psychoanalysis and the sociology of gender*. Berkeley: University of California Press.

Clark, M., Kaufman, S. & Pierce, R. (1976). Explorations of acculturation: Toward a model of ethnic identity. *Human Organization, 35*, 231-238.

Coleman, M. (1988). The division of household labor: Suggestions for future empirical consideration and theoretical development. *Journal of Family Issues, 9(1)*, 132-148.

Coleman, S. (1989, October 8). Quietly, community of Brazilians forms. *The Boston Globe*, p.1 (South Weekly).

Cooper, K., Chassin, L., Braver, S., Zeiss, A. & Khavari, K. (1986). Correlates of mood and marital satisfaction among dual-worker and single-worker couples. *Social Psychology Quarterly, 49(4)*, 322-329.

Cornelius, W. A. (1982). Interviewing undocumented immigrants: Methodological reflections based on fieldwork in Mexico and the U.S.. *International Migration Review, 16*, 378-411.

Cornille & Brotherton (1993). Applying the developmental family therapy model to issues of migrating families. *Marriage and family Review, 19(3/4)*, 325-340.

Costa, A.; Barroso, C. & Sarti, C. (1985). Pesquisa sobre mulher no Brasil: Do limbo ao gueto? *Cadernos de Pesquisa, 54*, 5-15.

Cuellar, I., Harris, L., and Jasso, R. (1980). An acculturation scale for Mexican American normal and clinical populations. *Hispanic Journal of Behavioral Sciences, 2(3)*, 199-217.

D'Amorim, M. (1988). Estereótipos de gênero em universitários. *Psicologia: Reflexão e crítica, 3(1/2)*, 3-11.

Danziger, K. (1974). The acculturation of Italian immigrant girls in Canada. *Behavioral journal of Psychology, 9(2)*, 129-137.

DeBiaggi, Sylvia Dantas (1992). *From Minas to Mass: A qualitative study of five Brazilian families in Boston.* Unpublished paper, Boston University.

DeBiaggi, Sylvia Dantas (1996). Mudança, crise e redefinição: As mulheres brasileiras lá fora. *Travessia: Revista do migrante, 26*, 24-26.

References

Dela-Coleta, M. F. (1991). Causas atribuidas ao sucesso e fracasso no casamento. *Psico, 22(2)*, 21-39.

Denmark, F., Shaw, J. & Ciali, S. (1985). The relationship among sex roles, living arrangements, and the division of household responsibilities. *Sex Roles, 12 (5/6)*.

Dyal, J. & Dyal, R. (1981). Acculturation, Stress and Coping. *International Journal of Intercultural Relations, 5*, 301-328.

Emigrante é a nova prioridade do Itamaraty (2000 June 18). *O Estado de São Paulo*, p. A17.

Falicov, C. J. (1995). Training to Think Culturally: A Multidimensional Comparative Framework. *Family Process, 34 (4)*, 373-388.

Fowlkes, M. (1987). Role combination and role conflict: Introductory perspective. In F. Crosby (ed.), *Spouse, parent, worker: On gender and multiple roles*. New Haven: Yale University Press.

Franklin, J.L. (1992, February 3). Homeland troubles bring Brazilian influx to region. *The Boston Globe*, p.1, 14.

Freyre, G. (1964). The patriarchal basis of Brazilian Society. In J. Mayer & R.W. Weatherhead (eds.), *Politics of change in Latin America* (pp.155-173). New York: F. A. Praeger.

Ghaffarian, S. (1987). The Acculturation of Iranians in the United States. *Journal of Social Psychology, 127(6)*, 565-571.

Gilbert, L. (1985). *Men in dual-career families: Current realities and future prospects.* Hillsdale, NJ: Lawrence Erlbaum Associates Publishers.

Gilbert, L. (1993). *Two careers, one family: The promise of gender equality.* Newbury Park, CA: Sage Publications.

Gilligan, C. (1982). *In a different voice: Psychological theory and women's development.* Cambridge: Harvard Univ. Press.

Goza, F. (1994). Brazilian immigration to North America. *International Migration Review, vol. 28(1)*, pp.136-152.

Guendelman, S. (1987). The incorporation of Mexican women in seasonal migration: A study of gender differences. *Hispanic Journal of Behavioral Sciences, 9(3)*, 245-264.

Gunter, N. & Gunter, B.G. (1990). Domestic division of labor among working couples. Does androgyny make a difference? *Psychology of Women Quarterly, 14,* 355-370.

Hahner, J. (1984). *Women in Brazil: Problems and perspectives.* State university of New York at Albany.

Hannasab, S. (1991). Acculturation and young Iranian women: Attitudes toward sex roles and intimate relationships. *Journal of Multicultural Counseling and Development, 19,* 11-21.

References

Hartman, M. & Hartman, H. (1986). International migration and household conflict. *Journal of Comparative Family Studies, vol. 17(1)*, 131-138.

Harwood, R., Miller, J. & Irizarry, N. (1995). *Culture and attachment: Perceptions of the child in context.* New York: Guilford Press.

Havighurst, R. J. & Moreira, J. R. (1965). *Society and education in Brazil.* Pittsburgh: University of Pittsburgh.

Heisler, M. (1995). *Brazilians in East Boston: A Demographic Description and Assessment of Health Status, Services Utilization, and Barriers to Access Health Care.* Unpublished paper, East Boston Neighborhood Health Center.

Hiller, D. & Philliber, W. (1982). The division of labor in contemporary marriage: Expectations perceptions, and performance. *Social Problems, 33*, 191-201.

Hochschild, Arlie (1990). *The second shift.* New York: Avon Books.

Hollingshead, A B. (1975). *Four factor index of social status.* Working paper. Yale University, New Haven, Conn. Photocopy.

Hondagneu-Sotelo, (1994). *Gendered Transitions: Mexican Experiences of Immigration.* Berkeley: University of California.

Hood, J. (1986). The Provider Role: Its meaning and measurement. *Journal of Marriage and the Family, 48*, 349-359.

Instituto Brasileiro de Geografia e Estatística – IBGE Demographic Census 2000 [Eletronic data file], Brazil.

Jovem deportado pelos EUA chega a São Paulo (2000 November 17). *O Estado de São Paulo*, p.7

Junni, S. & Grimm, D. W. (1993). Marital Satisfaction and Sex-Roles in a New York Metropolitan Sample. *Psychological Reports, 73*, 307-314.

Kirkland, J. (1984). Modernization of family values and norms among Armenians in Sydney. *Journal of Comparative Family Studies, 15(3)*, 355-372.

Klintowitz, J. (1996, April 3). Nossa gente lá fora. *Veja*, p. 26-29.

Kramer & Conoley (1992). *The eleventh mental measurements yearbook.* Lincoln: University of Nebraska Press.

Landale, N. & Ogena, N. (1993). Migration and union dissolution among Puerto Rican women. *International Migration Review, 29*, 671-692.

Levine, R. & West, L. (1979). Attitudes toward women in the United States and Brazil. *Journal of Social Psychology, 108 (2)*, 265-266.

References

Lucena, R. (1990, November 4). Aumenta exodo para Japao e Estados Unidos. *Folha de São Paulo*, p. C-3.

Luepnitz, D. (1988). *The family interpreted: Psychoanalysis, feminism and family therapy.* Harper Collins Publishers.

Lye & Biblarz (1993). The effects of attitudes toward family life and gender roles on marital satisfaction. *Journal of Family Issues, 14 (2)*, 157-188.

Margolis, M. (1989). A new ingredient in the "melting pot": Brazilans in New York city. *City and Society, 3*, pp. 179-188.

Margolis, Maxine (1994). *Little Brazil.* Princeton University Press.

Marin, B., Otero-Sabogal, R., & Perez-Stable, E. (1987). Development of a short acculturation scale for Hispanics. *Hispanic Journal of Behavioral Sciences, 9(2)*, 183-205.

Martes, Ana Cristina Braga (1996). Trabalhadoras Brasileiras em Boston. *Travessia: Revista do migrante*, 19-23.

Martes, A. (1999). *Brasileiros nos Estados Unidos: Um estudo sobre imigrantes em Massachusetts.* São Paulo: Paz e Terra.

Martes, A. (2001). Emigração brasileira: formação de mercados de consumo de produtos brasileiros no exterior. *Revista RAE, vol. 41*, número 1, Jan.-Março.

Massi, M. (1992). *Vida de mulheres: Cotidiano e imaginário*. Rio de janeiro: Imago editora.

Melville, M. (1978). Mexican Women Adapt to Migration. *International Migration Review, 12(2)*, 225-235.

Mena, F., Padilla, A. & Maldonado, M. (1987). Acculturative stress and specific coping strategies among immigrant and later generation college students. *Hispanic Journal of Behavioral Sciences, 9(2)*, 207-225.

Mendoza, R. (1989). An empirical scale to measure type and degree of acculturation in Mexican-American adolescents and adults. *Journal of Cross-cultural Psychology, 20(4)*, 372-385.

Mendoza, R. & Martinez, J. (1981). The measurement of Acculturation. In Barón (Ed.), *Explorations in Chicano psychology* (pp. 77-82). New York: Praeger publishers.

Meredith, W. & Rowe, G. (1986). Changes in Lao Hmong marital attitudes after immigrating to the United States. *Journal of Comparative Family Studies, 17(1)*, 117-126.

Miller, C. I. (1979). The function of middle-class extended family networks in Brazilian urban society. In M. L. Margolis & W. E. Carter (Eds.), *Brazil, anthropological perspectives* (pp. 305-316). New York: Columbia University Press.

Miller, J. (1986). *Towards a new psychology of women*. Boston: Beacon press.

References

Millman, J. (1997). *The other Americans: How immigrants renew our country, our economy, and our values.* New York: Viking.

Morokvasic, M. (1984). Birds of passage are also women ... *International Migration Review, 18(4)*, 886-907.

Morell, J. M. (1997). *Marital satisfaction: The contributions of cognitions, affect, and femininity.* Unpublished doctoral dissertation, Boston University, Massachusetts.

Naidoo, J. & Davis, J. (1988). Canadian South Asian women in transition: A dualistic view of life. *Journal of Comparative Families Studies, 19(2)*, 311-327.

Nguyen, T. (1995, August 6). U.S. Citizenship Becomes Their Goal. Campaign in Somerville Targets the Portuguese. *The Boston Globe*, p.4 (City Weekly).

O'Leary, V., Unger, R. & Wallston, B. (1985). *Women, Gender and Social Psychology.* New Jersey: Lawrence Erlbaum Ass. Publishers.

O povo da diaspora {The diaspora people} (1991, August 7). *Veja*, pp. 13-15.

Padilla, A. (1980). The role of cultural awareness and ethnic loyalty in acculturation. In A. Padilla (Ed.), *Acculturation: Theory, models, and some new findings.* Boulder: Westview Press, pp. 47-84.

Padilla, A, Wagatsuma, Y. & Lindholn, K. (1985). Acculturation and personality as predictors of stres in

Japanese and Japanese-Americans. *The Journal of Social Psychology, 125(3)*, 295-305.

Parrillo, V. (1991). The immigrant family: Securing the American dream. *Journal of Comparative Families Studies, 22(2)*, 131-145.

Peplau, L. & Gordon, S. (1985). Women and men in love: Gender differences in close heterosexual relationships. In O'Leary, Unger and Wallston (Eds.) *Women, Gender and Social Psychology* (pp. 257-291). New Jersey: Lawrence Erlbaum Ass. Publishers.

Peplau, L., Hill, C. & Rubin, Z. (1993). Sex Role Attitudes in Dating and Marriage: A 15 Year Follow-Up of the Boston Couples Study. *Journal of Social Issues, 49(3)*, 31-52.

Pessar, P. (1984). The linkage between the household and workplace of Dominican women in the U.S.. *International Migration Review, 18(4)*, 1188-1211.

Phineey, J.(1990). Ethnic identity in adolescents and adults: Review of research. *Psychological Bulletin, 108(3)*, 499-514.

Phinney, J., Chavira, V. & Williamson, L. (1992). Acculturation attitudes and self-esteem among high school and college students. *Youth and Society, 23(3)*, 299-312.

Pick-de-Weiss, S. (1981). Problems in the Administration of Questionnaires With Fixed-Response Format and Attitudinal Scales in a Developing Country.

References

Revista de la Asociacion Latinoamericana de Psicologia Social, 1, 57-62.

Pierson, D. (1954). The Family in Brazil. *Marriage and Family Living*, 16, 308-314.

Pina, D. & Bengtson, V. (1995). Division of household labor and the well-being of retirement aged wives. *The gerontologist*, 35 (3), 308-317.

Pleck, J. (1976). The male sex role: Definitions, problems, and sources of change. *Journal of Social Issues*, vol. 32(3), 155-164.

Pleck, J. (1985). *Working Wives / Working Husbands*. New York: Sage

Queralt, M. (1984). Understanding Cuban Immigrants: A Cultural Perspective. *Social Work*, 29, 115-121.

Radice, J. (1987). Papéis sexuais no nordeste do Brasil: sua desejabilidade e possíveis consequências para a autorealização da mulher. *Revista de Psicologia, 5,* 93-103.

Ramos, D. (1978). City and Country: The Family in Minas Gerais 1804-1838. *Journal of Family History, 3(4),* 361-375.

Ribeiro, G. (1999). O que faz o Brasil, Brazil: jogos identitários em São Francisco. In R.R. Reis & T. Sales (Eds.), *Cenas do Brasil migrante* (pp. 45-85)

Rogler, L., Cortes, D. & Malgady, R. (1991). Acculturation and Mental Health Status Among Hispanics. *American Psychologist, 46(6),* 585-597

Rohner, R. (1984). Toward a Conception of Culture for Cross-Cultural Psychology. *Journal of Cross-cultural psychology, 15(2),* 111-138.

Rosemberg, F. (1994). A Educacao de Mulheres Jovens e Adultas no Brasil. In H. I. B. Saffioti & M. Munoz-Vargas (Eds.), *Mulher Brasileira é Assim* (pp. 27-62). Rio de Janeiro: Rosa dos Tempos.

Rueschenberg, E. & Buriel, R. (1989). Mexican American Family Functioning and Acculturation: A Family Systems Perspective. *Hispanic Journal of Behavioral Sciences, 11(3),* 232-244.

Sa, H. T. (1947). *The Brazilians, People of Tomorrow.* New York: John Day Company.

Saffioti, H. I. B. (1984). Violencia de Genero no Brasil Contemporaneo . In H. I. B. Saffioti & M. Munoz-Vargas (Eds.), *Mulher brasileira é assim* (pp. 151-186). Rio de Janeiro: Rosa dos Tempos.

Salgado, E. & Carelli, G. (2001, July 18) Eles fogem da bagunça. *Veja,* p. 94-100.

Sarti, C. (1989). Reciprocidade e Hierarquia: Relações de Gênero na Periferia de São Paulo. *Cadernos de Pesquisa, 70,* 38-46.

References

Sales, A. (1984). *Pattern of community contact and Immigrant adjustment: A study of Soviet Jews in Boston.* Unpublished doctoral dissertation, Boston University, Massachusetts.

Sales, T. (1991). Novos fluxos migratórios da população brasileira. *Revista Brasileira de Estudos de Populacão, vol. 8, n.1/2*.

Scarr, S., Phillips, D. & McCartney, K. (1989). Working Mothers and Their Families. *American Psychologist, 44(11),* 1402-1409.

Scott, R. (1990) O Homem na Matrifocalidade; Gênero, Percepção e Experiências do Domínio Doméstico. *Cadernos de Pesquisa, 73,* 38-47.

Shuval, J. (1993). Migration and Stress. In L. Goldberger & S. Breznitz (eds.), *Handbook of stress: Theoretical and clinical aspects.* New York: The free press.

Skidmore, T. E. (1988). *The Politics of Military Rule in Brazil, 1964-85.* New York: Oxford University Press.

Sluski, C. E. (1979). Migration and Family Conflict. *Family Process, 18(4),* 379-390.

Sluski, C. (1997). *A rede social na prática sistêmica.* São Paulo: Casa do Psicólogo.

Soares, W. (1999). Emigração e (i)mobilidade residencial: momentos de ruptura na reprodução/ continuidade de segregação social no espaço urbano. In

R.R. Reis & T. Sales (Eds.), *Cenas do Brasil migrante* (pp. 167-193)

Spanier, G.B. (1976). Measuring Dyadic Adjustment: New Scales for Assessing the Quality of Marriage and Similar Dyads. *Journal of Marriage and the Family, 38*, 15-28.

Spence, J. T. & Hahn, E. (1997). The Attitudes Toward Women Scale and Attitude Change in College Students. *Psychology of Women Quarterly, 21*, 17-34.

Spence, J.T. & Helmreich, R. L. (1972). The attitudes toward women scale: An objective instrument of measure of attitudes towards the rights and roles of women in contemporary society. *Journal Supplement Abstract Service Catalog of Selected Documents in Psychology, 2*, 66-67.

Staples, R. & Mirande, A. (1980). Racial and Cultural Variations Among American families: A decennial review of the literature on minority families. *Journal of Marriage and the Family, 42*, 157-173.

Suárez-Orozco, C. & Suárez-Orozco, M. (1995). Transformations> Migration, family life, and achievement motivation among Latino adolescents. Stanford: Stanford University Press.

Suitor, J. (1991). Marital quality and satisfaction with the division of household labor across the family life cycle. *Journal of Marriage and the Family, 53*, 221-230.

References

Tomlinson, S. (2001, January 01). Local cable stations sharpen their focus: Immigrants seen as key audience. *The Boston Globe*, p.1 (City weekly).

Torres-Matrullo, C. (1976). Acculturation and Psychopathology among Puerto Rican women in mainland United States. *American Journal of Orthopsychiatry, 46(4)*, 710-719.

Torres-Matrullo, C. (1980). Acculturation, sex-role values and mental health among mainland Puerto Rican. In A. Padilla (ed.), *Acculturation:Theory, models, and some new findings* (pp. 11-137). Boulder: Westview Press.

Twenge, J.M.(1997). Attitudes toward women, 1970-1995. *Psychology of Women Quarterly, 21*, 35-51.

U.S. Immigration and Naturalization Service, *Statistical Yearbook of the Immigration and Naturalization Service*, 1998, U.S. Government Printing Office: Washington, D.C., 2000

Vigue, D. (1995, February 19). A Success Story in Marlborough. *The Boston Globe*, p.1 (West Weekly).

Wagley, C. (1963). *An introduction to Brazil.* New York: Columbia University Press.

Wagley, C. (1964). Luso-Brazilian kinship patterns: The Persistence of a Cultural Tradition. In J. Mayer & R. W. Weatherhead (eds.), *Politics of Change in Latin America* (pp. 175-189). New York: Frederick A. Praeger.

Walker, L. & Wallston, B. (1985). Social adaptation: A review of dual-earner family literature. In L. L'Abate (Ed.), *The handbook of family psychology*. Homewood, Illinois: The Dorsey Press.

Winstead, B. & Derlega, V. (1993). Gender and Close Relationships: An Introduction. *Journal of Social Issues, 49(3)*, 1-9.

Woon, Y. (1986). Some adjustment aspects of Vietnamese and Sino-Vietnamese families in Victoria, Canada. *Journal of Comparative Family Studies, 17(3)*, 349-370.

Wong, B. (1985). Family, kinship, and ethnic identity of the Chinese in New York city, with comparative remarks on the Chinese in Lima, Peru and Manila, Philippines. *Journal of Comparative Families Studies, 16*, 231-254.

Zammichieli, M., Gilroy, F. & Sherman, M. (1988). Relation Between Sex-Role Orientation and Marital Satisfaction. *Personality and Social Psychology Bulletin, 14(4)*, 747-754.

Index

Abortion, 55
abusive relationships, 101
Acculturative stress, 33
American family households, 107
Assimilation, 28
average age of the husbands, 63
average age of the wives, 63
awareness, 29, 159
Berry, 25, 27, 29, 30, 33, 34, 41, 104, 147, 148
bicultural perspective, 26
bilingual Portuguese-English programs, 21
Brazilian family, 50, 51, 150
Brazilian legislation, 56
Brazilian organizations, 22
Brazilian sample's characteristics, 106
Canada, 13, 30, 31, 60, 152, 166
characteristics of subordinates, 40
child care, 40, 42, 58, 96, 128
childcare tasks, 69, 74, 78, 80, 81, 82, 87, 88, 90, 91
cleaners, 4
clinical implications, 113
cluster analysis, 91, 95, 96

coping, 33, 34, 36, 37, 157
crisis situation, 35
cultural, 2, 4, 10, 17, 22, 23, 24, 25, 26, 27, 28, 29, 30, 32, 33, 34, 39, 41, 45, 70, 77, 100, 102, 104, 105, 107, 112, 113, 125, 146, 148, 158, 159, 162
cultural change, 25, 26, 104, 105
culture, 1, 2, 5, 12, 16, 17, 23, 24, 25, 26, 27, 28, 29, 31, 33, 37, 39, 58, 100, 107, 110, 111, 114, 150
culture of out-migration, 12
Deculturation, 27
domestic violence, 56
double moral standard, 52
downward mobility, 32, 60
ethnic identification, 77
ethnic loyalty, 29, 159
exchange theory, 43
extended family, 15, 114, 115, 158
familism, 114, 115
father's permission, 111
female citizenship, 56
feminine household tasks, 68, 74, 79, 81, 83, 87, 88, 91, 98, 109

Feminist ideology, 43
government policies, 7, 30
Grinberg and Grinberg, 35
Hispanic, 1, 151, 154, 157, 158, 162
Hondagneu-Sotelo, 59, 106, 115, 155
Hoschild, 45
host society, 27, 29
house, 4, 18, 20, 54, 65, 66, 68, 79, 101, 107, 110, 128, 133, 139
housecleaners, 64, 100
housecleaners for American families, 64
husband's marital satisfaction, 109
immigrant families, 1, 3, 4, 15, 58, 59, 70, 72, 103, 104, 106, 108, 113, 114, 116
immigration to Brazil, 7
Integration, 28
interaction terms, 84, 86
Jean Baker Miller, 39
Latin, 101, 114, 115, 116, 153, 165
Latino population, 1
liberal gender roles, 46, 73
linear model, 26
Luepnitz, 41, 156
male magical strength, 40
Margolis, 1, 12, 14, 17, 19, 41, 42, 157, 158
marital dissolution, 3, 104
marital satisfaction, 5, 48, 49, 61, 67, 71, 73, 74, 75, 80, 83, 84, 85, 86, 87, 88, 96, 97, 103, 108, 109, 115, 150, 151, 156

masculine household tasks, 68, 74, 79, 81, 83, 87, 90, 98
masculinity, 47, 48, 51, 53, 114
Melting Pot, 28
Minas Gerais, 11, 13, 15, 16, 52, 64, 161
modes of acculturation, 27
motherhood, 41
Multiple regression analyses, 84
Nancy Chodorow, 39
New York, 8, 9, 10, 14, 17, 23, 148, 149, 150, 153, 154, 155, 157, 158, 161, 162, 163, 165, 166
oppressive position, 111
outcome measures, 84
patriarchal society, 51, 103
personal contact, 115
Phinney, 25, 26, 104, 160
Portes, 19, 21
Portuguese family, 50
Pressure Cooker, 28
psychological, 2, 23, 25, 33, 40, 41, 67
pull factors, 20
push factors, 19
Qualitative Results, 99
Rejection, 27
remittances, 12, 13
resource theory, 43
role differentiation theory, 44
Roles, V, 39, 152, 155
Ryan-Einot-Gabriel-Welsch multiple range test of means, 94, 95, 98
salaries per week, 65
sample education, 63
Sluski, 36, 38, 57, 163

Index

social networks, 18, 21, 23, 36
specific hypotheses, 72
stress, 15, 31, 33, 36, 47, 58, 105, 147, 157, 163
study questionnaire designed, 65
Suarez-Orozco, VII, 2, 38
surveys on time, 44
time in U.S, 78, 93, 95
traditional attitudes towards women, 68
Traditional gender roles, 47
traditional marriages, 32
traditional sex role ideology, 45
transnational migration, 19
traumatic experience, 35
tubal ligations, 55
TV Globo, 22
unity of the family, 114
upward mobility, 32
women's double shift, 105

Printed in the United States
31799LVS00001B/31-42